Landscapes – of Poverty

NATIONAL
LOTTERY
CHARITIES
BOARD

This book was produced with assistance from ACRE
(Action with Communities in Rural England) as part
of their Rural Poverty Initiative, and part financed with
funds from the National Lottery Charities Board.

Landscapes – of Poverty

Aspects of rural England in the late 1990s

Michael Simmons

Also by Michael Simmons

Berlin: The Dispossessed City (Hamish Hamilton, 1988)
The Unloved Country (Abacus Original, 1989)
The Reluctant President: A Political Life of Vaclav Havel
(Methuen, 1991)

Michael Simmons, currently Deputy Editor of the Society section of *The Guardian*, has spent most of his journalistic career writing for quality British newspapers about social and economic developments in Britain and Europe.

After a period on the Parliamentary staff of the *Glasgow Herald*, he joined the *Financial Times* where he was Soviet and East Europe Correspondent for several years before transferring to *The Guardian* and taking up the same position. In between, he was the first editor of the *Guardian Third World Review*, which became a significant forum for discussion of third world issues, and co-edited a book of features from the *Review*'s pages, *Voices from the South* (Hodder & Stoughton).

He played the leading part in *The Guardian*'s coverage of East Europe's anti-communist revolutions. He has written a full-length political history of Berlin and, shortly before its demise, a political "profile" of the GDR, and in, 1991, a biography of Vaclav Havel, published also in German and Czech.

Between times, he has written for *The Guardian*'s arts and travel pages and other feature pages. He has also written for the *New Statesman* and for the Rowntree Foundation journal, *Search*.

Michael Simmons, born in 1935, is a Manchester University honours graduate in German and Russian. He is married to a Scottish social worker and has two grown up sons.

First published in Great Britain 1997 by Lemos & Crane
20 Pond Square
Highgate Village
London N6 6BA

Published in association with
ACRE (Action with Communities in Rural England)
Somerford Court
Somerford Road
Cirencester
Glos. GL7 1TW

ISBN 1-898001-38-3

A CIP catalogue record for this book is available from the
British Library

Design and formatting by Digital Artworks Partnership Ltd, London

Printed and bound by Redwood Books, Trowbridge.

Contents

Acknowledgements

this book was commissioned by Les Roberts, director of ACRE (Action with Communities in Rural England) who in late 1996 received funding from the National Lottery Charities Board specifically for the purpose. He has let me write my own book, for which I am very grateful, as I am for the additonal guidance and encouragement received from him, from Nicky Philpott (until she left), Mark Richardson and from many other ACRE people.

Specialist help and authoritative knowledge from Gillian Kempster and others at the Rural Development Commission; from Lisa Harker, Audrey Bronstein, Charles Marsden, Paul Milbourne, May Molteno, Howard Newby, Katie Prince, Brian Shucksmith, Denise Servante, Helen Sudlow, Diana Walkden, Caroline Welch, and a host of others was invaluable.

Busy people at the Rural Community Councils, for whom ACRE is the umbrella organisation, were generous with their time and kind enough to answer a series of fact-seeking questions I asked them early on: their pertinent answers appear throughout the text.

Paul Crane, publisher, and David Clare, an editor with very clear attitudes, provided much appreciated guidance and pleasant company to work with. I am also grateful to David Brindle, Social Services Correspondent, and John Vidal, Environment Editor – both good friends and colleagues at *The Guardian* – who read and helpfully commented on the manuscript. Malcolm Dean, with whom I work on *Guardian Society*, gave me the time to indulge my enthusiasm for things rural. Cathy Cover and *The Guardian*'s information technology team, always willing to help, shared indispensable skills.

But special thanks go to Angela, Stephen and Lys Williams, and Alastair Simmons – all, in their way, insightful sociologists. Each of them was extraordinarily helpful in all sorts of ways.

By Way of Foreword

Ironically, it was at the start of the 1997 grouse season, when the rurally-based well-to-do set off with guns for their ritual "country pursuits", that the Blair Government announced it was setting up a task force to investigate poverty. Only a few weeks before, a mass rally in London had been held in support of field sports on the grounds that they were essential components of the rural economy.

The ministerial announcement, delivered even as the first grouse were reaching their allotted dinner tables, said the Prime Minister himself would preside over harnessing the full power of government to tackle "the greatest social crisis of our times". This was "the scourge and the waste of social exclusion". Not surprisingly, there were sceptical and critical reactions: it was as if the Millennium had come three years too soon.

Many people, when the announcement was made, had never been better off – but there was also ample evidence that poverty, and the gap between rich and poor, had been growing in recent years at an unprecedented rate. Ministers, furthermore, and those reacting to them, seemed to be thinking, if not on wrong, then on distorted premises. Their thinking was on the well-trodden paths of the inner cities and deprived urban areas.

In fact, there is also evidence that hundreds of thousands, if not millions, who are poor live – and wait – in the countryside. They reserve judgement, cynically or otherwise, on the task force until they can taste the pudding it produces. They have been waiting many years, and it is to them that this book is dedicated.

Michael Simmons
London
August 1997

Chapter *one*
What You See

The face of our countryside is fair and prosperous. Our lanes are full of Range Rovers. Our country cottages have been improved into residences that sell for astronomical sums, and so have our ancient barns, and sometimes our churches and chapels. Millionaires buy entire Scottish islands. The pony-riding tribe of fortunate daughters parades every Saturday and Sunday morning. Ramblers in lividly bright, expensive garments – designed to insulate them against any experience of country weather — trudge along our footpaths. But one in four or five of people who live in these playgrounds is in poverty. The Minister responsible for the White Paper that ignored poverty is the Secretary of State for the Environment....

The Countryman, Vol 101, No 2.Spring 1996.
Editorial, by Christopher Hall

to the urban sentimentalist, it is the apparently unchanging character of the English countryside which appeals. To the restless country-dweller, it is the bright lights and the ill-defined "opportunities" of the town or the big city. On the eve of the millennium, the English way of life is such that, on a summer's morning, motorised individuals from the rural areas will join rush-hour traffic jams to reach their place of work, being passed in the opposite direction by townspeople on their way to the countryside in a collective bid "to get away from it all".

Ironically, it is not beyond plausibility that the commuter now heading into town is someone who emigrated some years ago to live "in the country". The townies travelling countrywards were themselves born, or their parents were born, in a rural area, perhaps not a million miles from the spot which is now their destination.

The countryside itself is as unamenable to definition as the individuals who inhabit it. For those aligning themselves with the heritage lobby it was acclaimed (in 1990) as "mankind's supreme contribution to the beauty of this planet". For Jamie Uplands, who lives on his wits and a bit of poaching in a Wiltshire village of 300, it barely exists at all. "No village life, no community, it's all gone," he told an interviewer called May Molteno in 1993. "We try so hard to make things up ... barbecues, anything. Nobody'll join. It's all gone now. All country craft's gone."

For the neutral observer, this intractability becomes apparent if he or she goes to the same vantage point in different seasons of the year. This observer, if he is lucky, will discern something of mankind's "supreme contribution". But then, if he looks hard enough, he will also uncover some underlying secrets, aspects of a rural life which most nostalgists and most central policy-makers tend to ignore.

You, reader, can be that observer. Choose a day when the English summer is at its bracing best and take a trip, if you're willing to risk the nose-to-tail driving experience, to the Cotswolds, the Derbyshire Peaks, the Lake District, the South Downs or the Suffolk coast, and an inescapable fact-of-life of rurality in England today will confront you. Pubs, tea-rooms, craft centres and car parks will be full; churches will be besieged by visitors – though rarely by worshippers – and all the ruined castles, ancient abbeys and historic houses – homes no longer – will be quietly overrun by paying guests.

These are known as the honey-pots. It is in such buildings, in such places, that the tills – in the words of a well-satisfied Countryside Commission (1996) – are "jingling" to the tune of literally billions of pounds.

But then come back again on a wet, uncrowded day in sombre November or a cold one in dank February. The only visible evidence of the encroaching greenhouse effect is a late, very late, blossom, perhaps a weather-beaten rose or two, and precious little else. You will find lots of space in the car park, but the tea-rooms, craft centres and historic houses will almost certainly be closed and possibly boarded up against unwelcome intruders. Happily, the pub will be open, even if the food and the service are pale shadows of their summer selves.

The "grandeur" which characterised the scenery in the spring, summer and colourful autumn months has given way to a bleakness which is less than welcoming. Whither is fled, as the poet asked, the visionary gleam? What price, after all, the "unchanging character" of the countryside?

But this too is rural England. For all its innate contradictions and the inconsistency of its "attractions", this is the environment which is home to more than one in four of the country's population. In 1971, 11 million people – out of a total, for England, of 46.5 million – lived in the rural areas. A quarter of a century later, the rural proportion was 13.4 million out of a total of nearly 49 million. The rural "slice" of the whole has gone up in size by around 20 per cent, while the whole had only grown by something like four per cent.

These are the people who have either lived in the countryside from birth or have chosen, at a relatively late stage in their lives, to put down roots "in the country". On the evidence of surveys carried out in recent years, they can expect to be joined sooner rather than later by more than four million others who say they have plans to move to the country by the end of the decade. Another 8 million or so have said they would do the same if they had the opportunities and the resources. Either way, the rural population is expected to grow considerably faster than the population of England as a whole.

Given such perceptions and such wishful thinking, it will take a lot of re-thinking to do away with the rural idyll – part heritage and part confidence trick – which so many of us take for granted. Almost certainly, it is so deep-rooted that it never will be destroyed. It has been in the mind, and described on paper, at least since the times of Ancient Greece.

In England, it has for centuries been cherished and encouraged, wittingly and unwittingly, by poets, painters and musicians. More recently, it has become a nice little earner for hundreds of tour operators and a whole range of hoteliers large and small within Britain and from overseas. Accidents of geology which have become known, and loved, as "the English landscape" – areas, perhaps, of outstanding natural beauty – have become very precious to the human psyche.

Where would English painting or literature be without those who have depicted the countryside? Where would a very lucrative section of the greetings card industry be without a thoroughly predictable nostalgia for the cottages and the peasantry of Victorian England? What would it do for the "business" of the National Trust, the Council for the Protection of Rural England, the Countryside Commission, and countless other concerned lobbies and vested interests, if the bright and beautiful things which have for so long given them sustenance were suddenly expunged?

This idyll does, of course, carry elements of a reality in its own right. Pretty cottages do exist, just as happy peasants and apple-cheeked farmers also exist, and children do play happily on the village green. But the idyll is only a part of a hugely complicated whole. How big a part varies from person to person, according to his or her perceptions.

Beauty is in the eye of the beholder, which is a way of saying that the joys of living in the countryside today are not by any means the same for everyone out there. For some, they may hardly even exist. "One person's splendid isolation was another's loneliness," said the compilers of an important survey of *Lifestyles in Rural England*, published by the Rural Development Commission in 1994. "The close-knit community for many can be the prying, gossiping intrusion for others. Some of these factors are largely in the realm of individual psychological responses to the locale, but others appeared to be part of a more inter-connected form of marginalisation."

This survey broke new ground for those concerned with attitudes to the English rural scene, and I shall draw frequently and with gratitude from its findings and contents in the pages that follow. Late 1990s Britain is at a socially fascinating time in its history and no book treating on a countryside theme could be seriously undertaken without some recourse to the evidence turned up by the compilers the survey.

But what do these researchers mean when they talk of marginalisation? What, one wonders, would the word mean to the farmers living in and around the Lake District who were asked, in early 1996, if they would desist from mixing and spreading manure during Bank holidays and weekends as the smell was offensive to visitors? Or what would it signify for the Devonshire owner of Corky the cockerel (cited in the RDC's *Lifestyles* survey), who was taken to court by his neighbours in the village of Stoke in a bid to halt what they considered the unacceptable "noise" of Corky's crowing? Or what would those inhabitants of the Derbyshire market town of Bakewell say if they had lost the epic struggle they had to go through in the mid-1990s to get their cattle market rebuilt on a nearby greenfield site? Their plans, which can only boost the local economy, went through in defiance of others who lived in or were regular visitors to the same town and who had protested that the development would "spoil" the special character of this particular Peak District attraction.

Such clashes of interest occur as a matter almost of routine in many parts of rural England – the Bakewell project did excite exceptionally strong feelings on both sides – and they are occurring with increasing frequency. This is not just because the population of the countryside has been growing in recent years; it is also because this population represents a widening variety of interests. There is a new, very 20th-century breed of country people: "the incomers".

These are people who may arrive and settle, in some ways rather as their forebears, the so-called Empire "builders", may have settled in more distant corners of the old colonies in the last century or early in the present one. But then, in other ways they emphatically do not resemble the Empire builders. The latter, after all, used to fantasise about the English countryside as they languished on their tropical verandahs – though theirs was a countryside dominated perhaps by the great country houses their own forebears may have built with colonial earnings.

Today's settlers in rural England come with the best will in the world, but they may arrive with no real understanding of what they are taking on in the way of prevailing lifestyles, customs and traditions. Life in the country village of the late 20th century has little in common with life as it was lived in English country houses in their prime.

Clearly, something of the rural idyll, or "culture", has drawn them there as much as any notion of economic expediency or of the apparent lack of stress and the supposedly healthy air. Even some fashionable notion of "wilderness" in the locality may have been influential. Some or all of this may have appeared very congenial and even seductive at first reading – say, in the houses-for-sale columns of the local press, or as members of the family sat enjoying a July picnic in a green meadow by a stream, with the grazing cattle and their "mess" conveniently out of harm's way on the other bank.

Possibilities that, as incomers, they might turn out to be the ones who would sooner or later become excluded or somehow marginalised from the rural round in which they wanted to become immersed are possibilities they choose either to suppress or to keep to themselves. Perhaps they say to themselves, with a sort of managed respect, that it won't happen to them. Tinted spectacles can have their uses: the blemishes in the picture are not so visible.

The prime concern of this book is only peripherally with people such as these, though their plight does emerge intermittently as a matter of real and very relevant interest. The main focus will be on millions of others who are living distinctly unsentimental lives on what can only be called the margins. These people are the rural poor and the deprived, and they may be counted victims of a new kind of poverty which may have little to do with the land.

It may be considered indecent or discordant to focus on such people in the context of what one distinguished (and highly controversial) rural lobbyist, Marion Shoard (*The Theft of the Countryside*, London, 1980), has depicted as "a vital part of our national identity, (which) for hundreds of years has given us such ideas as we have had of what paradise might be like". But they too are as real – and therefore just as important if the picture of today's countryside is to be complete – as anything that can be conjured up by the idyll.

These are people, sometimes disparagingly referred to as the "underclass", who emerge only occasionally as subjects for political debate. They barely managed to get look-in during the general election campaigns of the 1980s and 1990s. The poor, in urban as well as country areas, but especially in the countryside, have become a widening layer at the bottom of society of increasing, if covert, concern to policy-makers. It will be a test of the claims to humanity of the New Labour administration to see how far it goes in meeting the needs of the poor.

Ministers in the Government which was so unceremoniously swept out of office in May 1997, did very little in this direction. In the last months before that election took place, ministers had gone out of their way to deny that poverty even existed in 1990s Britain. It was as if they had been presented with a dilemma which they seemed, and still seem, unable fully to comprehend.

Poverty in the traditionally deeply-loved "green and pleasant" countryside has been something especially difficult for policy-makers of the 1980s and the first half of the 1990s to take in. The argument from the political Right has been that, in the last quarter of the 20th century, social and economic change has led to increased incomes for the majority and improved standards of living. Despite being saddled with the biggest Social Security budget in history, and with areas of the country where unemployment and/or insecurity of employment have become bread-and-butter issues, the Right has paid voluble lip service to the notion, voiced by John Major when he became Prime Minister, that Britain should be a nation "at ease with itself". It was a notion which many used as a sort of armour against the slings and arrows of outraged oppositionists.

Of course, some individual local authorities, pressure groups and charities with rural responsibilities have expressed concern. A handful of them have worked at the problems very conscientiously – from few real resources. Some local authorities went as far as setting up their own strategy units to examine rural poverty and to report their findings to members of Parliament and to ministers. In doing so, they have sometimes been politically short-changed, told that their definitions and their criteria were wrong, that they were distorting "facts" to back a misdirected argument, and that, since things were getting better anyway, they should go away and think of something else.

Central and local government leaders have grown used to being on opposite sides of the negotiating table, but politicians who have responded in this way have inadvertently exacerbated the polarisation – between the haves and the have-nots – that has been accentuated in Britain over the last quarter of a century. This is a theme to which I shall return later. So far as the countryside is concerned, such inherently unhelpful responses have also done their bit to protect the idyll.

But, politics aside, the English – in the words of the Countryside Commission (January-February 1996) – are engaged in "a love affair" with their countryside. This is in spite of, perhaps even because of, the fact that Britain, as its central government acknowledges, is one of the most urbanised countries in Europe. England, the focus for this particular book, is the most urbanised part of the United Kingdom.

Rural England's "vulnerability", according to the London policy-makers, stems in large measure from the fact that is so easily accessible. There is hardly a spot in England, said a keynote report from the Government's white paper of 1995, *Rural England: A Nation Committed to a Living Countryside*, that would not fall within city limits if it were in the US, and hardly a farm which is more than 30 miles from a major town or city.

A poll, conducted by the Countryside Commission at about the time this particular report was going to press, confirmed that nine people out of every 10 valued the countryside as "an important part of our heritage". They declared that it had to be be protected, as "a moral duty" and "at all costs", for future generations.

Day trippers, said the Commission, were spending around £6,000 million a year in country shops, pubs, garages, leisure attractions and other "rural enterprises" in the course of well over 1,000 million visits a year to the countryside. "It is important," declared Roger Clarke, the Commission's director of policy, in the wake of the survey, "that money continues to be invested in keeping the countryside beautiful".

Such thinking begs some central questions: whose countryside is it anyway, and who, outside the parameters of the personal enthusiasms and the vested interests already cited, can say whether or not there is still a coherent rural English way of life? Assuming some sort of stab can be made in that direction, other questions arise. Who is to assess, and how, the existence and the nature of poverty and deprivation which are an undeniable part of that way of life?

Action with Communities in Rural England (ACRE) was formed in 1987. It is a product of the expanding industry of concern relating to the countryside which has been evolving throughout the 20th century and, in the latter part of the century, at a strikingly accelerated pace. ACRE's emergence and steadily rising profile have coincided with shifts in population towards the countryside, and with the raising of pertinent questions about the way other people live there.

The well-heeled have shown with their feet, and with the easing of their purse-strings, that they are willing to pay high prices (high in rural terms) for roses round the door, with or without a plot of land, while still maintaining their business, shopping and cultural links with the nearest town or city. At the same time, ACRE has taken it upon itself to campaign, with voluntary backing from all parts of the country, against the impoverishment and the already measurable poverty which have afflicted people who, in some instances, have been living in the countryside all their lives.

Within the span of its first decade, ACRE has become recognised as a leading charity which has an in-built nuisance potential for deci-sion-takers and policy-makers. Most crucially, it has been at its best in this role when monitoring the incidence of persisting disadvantage in rural England and when generating some fierce debates on the issues thrown up. It is partly funded by, and operates in association with, the Rural Development Commission but spends most of its proactive time working with and for communities and their represen-tative councils, usually at county level. Its director, symptomatically, is not a career civil servant but a former social worker, Les Roberts.

ACRE has not hesitated to examine in close-up the under-belly of rural England, exposing the lack of amenity and the poor quality of life of many who live there. Its activities – like those of, say, Shelter in the field of housing and homelessness – have not always been to the taste of the Establishment or of the new and often affluent breed of country-dweller, but they have tended to be unremitting. The organisation has gone down and beyond the leafy lanes to open the lid of rural England. In doing so, it has been able to demonstrate that there are things that have more in common with those of Pandora's box than those of the proverbial chocolate box.

Chapter *two*
What You Don't See

*The pre-industrial economy had its own forms of dirt,
ugliness and social tensions, less obvious through lurking
in villages and cottages, but no less brutalising and
depressing to the human spirit than the environment of
the factory town.*

L.A. Clarkson,
The Pre-Industrial Economy in England, London 1971.

*There is now no party of the poor. At the bottom of the
heap, life is harder than at any time since the war. But
the bottom of the heap has no political clout.*

Lord (Roy) Hattersley, speaking in March 1997,
after more than 32 years as a member of the House of Commons

poverty is easier to identify than it is to define – though a number of definitions will be discussed later in this chapter. Income support payments are supposed to be the minimum that Parliament thinks necessary for recipients to live on. Figures published by the Government in the second half of the 1990s have shown a spectacular increase in poverty in almost all parts of the country; and the number making claims can be seen as one semi-official way of measuring and defining poverty.

The 1996 total had risen steeply to almost 6 million, more than 18 per cent up on the already high figure for early 1992. Interested politicians seized these figures and said they were the equivalent of nearly 900 new claimants every working day over the preceding four years – this even though the figures did not include the millions who, for a variety of reasons, failed to claim their entitlements. The unclaimed total was put at around £3 billion in 1994-95.

One of the sets of figures most commonly used in official circles, that measuring households below average income (HBAI), takes the total even higher. The HBAI returns in 1996 showed that a quarter of the country's population – more than 14 million people – were living on less than 50 per cent of average income after housing costs. This included more than 4 million children – one child in every three in Britain. Three-quarters of these children were living in families where there were no full-time workers.

In the last days of the 1997 general election campaign, the European Anti-Poverty Network, which consists of more than 200 voluntary organisations and community groups, threw its own small bombshell into the rather lethargic debate. Announcing that 14 million people in Britain were now living in poverty, it called on European institutions to set goals for cutting unemployment and combating poverty and social exclusion within the convergence criteria for a single European currency.

At the same time, it became apparent that the British Government had been suppressing statistics relating to poverty in our time. These came from the Child Poverty Action Group (CPAG) in London, and were later to be endorsed by the European Union statistics agency. They showed that Britain had more children living in poverty – one in every three – than any other European country. Only Portugal, of all the EU member states, had more adults and children below the poverty line than Britain. Evidence also accumulated from the United Nations, the Organisation for Economic Co-operation and Development, as well as some of the sitting Government's own statistical offices, which showed Britain to be an increasingly unequal society. No industrial country, apart from New Zealand, had seen such a dramatic increase in the size of the chasm between rich and poor.

The evidence was irrefutable. Indeed, as the CPAG argues, it had been for some time. These were officially authorised statistics, from a range of impeccable sources, and they stood as an indictment of seemingly complacent British attitudes on the eve of the millennium. Special pleading on behalf of the nation's poor had somehow been fudged or dismissed as rudely intrusive. For, during discussions on the progress of advanced national economies, the counter-argument would still be heard – that inequality is somehow acceptable, even "a stimulant to competition and an incentive".

In the 1980s, wrote Ian Gilmour, a former senior Minister of the time (and of whom more later), the Thatcherites fell back on another dogma: they blamed unemployment on the unemployed, so removing them from the category of "the deserving poor". But later, a Cabinet Minister, Peter Lilley, brazenly suggested in 1996 that poverty was a matter for them (the societies of the so-called Third World) rather than us (in the front rank of the First World) with our level of advanced technological sophistication. When Lilley voiced these words, he was a man of some substance in the Government of the day. But he gave this view not many months after an international aid worker had publicly announced that, in the experienced view of Oxfam, deprivation in parts of Britain bore a remarkable resemblance to deprivation in some Third World countries.

Since the early 1990s, Oxfam has been working on its own specific programme to alleviate poverty in contemporary Britain. The 1997 change in the complexion of the Government in Whitehall had no discernible impact on the shape or scope of this programme.

The word "underclass" is sometimes contentiously invoked to describe those whose lives might seem irreparable to many types of social engineer. It is a term which, according to the CPAG in 1996, expresses "more about the fears of the rest of society than about the reality it seeks to describe". For some, it may conjure up – if only for a moment – images of the "feckless" individuals about whom even the most philanthropic Victorians could feel distinctly uneasy. For a brief period in recent years, however, it became a term which provoked a highly diversionary, and therefore largely phoney, debate conducted from within the portals of the self-regarding Institute for Economic Affairs.

In 1996, Elaine Kempson, of the London-based Policy Studies Institute, examined in depth a series of studies which had been commissioned by the Rowntree Foundation. She was emphatic that people living on low incomes were not an underclass. They had aspirations just like the rest of us, she said, and they too wanted a job, a decent home, and an income that was enough to pay the bills and leave a little to spare. But life was difficult for them, their numbers were growing, and "fairly modest aspirations are often beyond their reach".

So what exactly is poverty? In its absolute form, it was defined by the United Nations, at a special world summit held in Copenhagen in March 1995, as "a condition characterised by severe deprivation of basic human needs, including food, safe drinking water, sanitation facilities, health, shelter, education and information. It depends not only on income but also on access to services."

At that meeting, Britain – while wearing diplomatic clothes – signed a declaration, along with 116 other international representatives, to eradicate poverty "through decisive national actions and international co-operation, as an ethical, social, political and economic imperative of humankind". A couple of years on, one can only assume the gesture was little more than an act of supreme cynicism. It promised "fully" to involve people who were living in poverty in setting targets and implementing national strategies. A review of progress is scheduled to be undertaken by the UN in the year 2000. One can already hear very important First World people gnashing their teeth and see them wringing their hands at the appalling lack of progress.

But how is the UN's description of absolute poverty applicable in rural England today? One place not to look for an answer to such a

In Dorset:
"Dorset is one of the worst counties for the provision of post offices, shops, transport, pubs, etc. Only three out of 12 market towns have a Job-Centre or benefit agency. Accident and Emergency services are only available at Weymouth or Poole. Rural doctors and pharmacies serve very large areas."

question was the White Paper put out by the British Government at the end of 1995, *Rural England, A Nation Committed to a Living Countryside*. Coming some six months after the Copenhagen declaration, ministers declared with some pride that it was the first such document to be published by a British Government since the end of the Second World War.

Others were more sceptical. Critics were quick to note that the White Paper took little account of people in specific age groups, such as children, teenagers, or young or old adults. It made no mention of marginalised groups, such as those on low incomes, of ethnic minorities, travellers, or the disabled. Christopher Hall, editor of *The Countryman*, usually a pleasant little journal for those who live more comfortably in the rural environment, went further. He declared angrily that the White Paper was "disgusting" and dismissed it as a "mishmash of pretty pictures and platitudes", saying that it was "stuffed full of guff about enterprises, partnerships and flexible and innovative approaches". There was not even a mention, he said, of the common euphemism for poverty – deprivation.

The 1997 general election campaign saw some lip service paid to the poor. The incoming Prime Minister, Tony Blair, from a well-heeled Scottish professional family, spoke movingly on arrival in office of uniting the country, of working for "the whole of society", even, in his programme, of doing something tangible to alleviate poverty. His words drew applause; his subsequent actions drew some scepticism.

John Major, the poor boy who, as he had insistently reminded us, had fought through family bankruptcy and the dole (briefly) to become Prime Minister, announced that – despite the 18 years of opportunities missed by the outgoing regime – his party still intended "to make haves of the have-nots". It was, however, a selective wish: the prime beneficiaries in financial terms of a series of financial proposals announced on the same occasion would have been those who were already in relatively comfortable circumstances. Families in which there was no one with a job would not qualify, nor where a single parent was head of household, nor where couples were living together but not married. A colleague on *The Guardian* said in the paper's leader column that this provision was neither a springboard nor even a safety net: it was Poor Law relief all over again.

But, regardless almost of political affiliations, such prescriptions from the policy-makers (as opposed to newspaper leader-writers) fell on sympathetic ears. A very substantial number of people in Britain had prospered on the back of the right-wing philosophies that had become their yardstick since the end of the 1970s. Poverty had grown dramatically, but social and economic attitudes had also changed. Those who were poor were having an increasingly rough time.

In the words of professional social workers (in a research report published in 1994), low income families in England could be divided into four categories. There were those who were keeping their heads above water; those who were sinking; those who were struggling to the surface; and those who were drowning. The slide into debt, said the researchers, was a much speedier process than the climb back to the surface.

Of course, there was rural poverty in England long before 1997 or the publication of the supposedly historic White Paper. Only the extent of it has been a matter of intense debate for social and political historians for generations. The political Right, up to and including the present period, has persistently argued by implication that if there has been, or still is, poverty in the countryside then it is essentially temporary in character. Anyway, some of them add, the "opportunities" offered by successive administrations suggest many of the poor have only themselves to blame for not seizing them with both hands.

The political Left has had no truck with this – claiming that the poor have been victims all along – of feudalism and the class system in the past, and the lack of genuinely viable opportunities in the present. Outside the ranks of the polemicists, however, no one has seriously doubted the realities of existing poverty. There has been no shortage of well-placed observers to claim that poverty in Britain has never been higher than it is now. It is there and it is measurable, they say, in pockets of the countryside, just as it is in the new ghettos of the inner cities. The God-fearing among the policy-makers and opinion-formers know. They have seen nothing to dissuade them from the Good Book's message that not only are the poor always with us, but they are also spiritually deserving people.

It is not difficult to trace the historical outlines and some of the origins of today's rural poverty. In the early 16th century, up to half the populations of the (then) small towns of Coventry, Exeter and Leicester were so poor that they were exempted from paying taxes. But this was a time when prices went up quickly and a Poor Law had to be introduced to alleviate spreading hardship. By the end of the 17th century, half the country's population – and sometimes more than that – were said to be running the risk of pauperdom from time to time. Under-employment and poor productivity characterised the agricultural scene.

In the countryside, the enclosure programme, which had already been going on for centuries, had accelerated and led to a sharp increase in the numbers of dispossessed, landless and impoverished families. As Clarkson has noted, many had depended on the common lands, now lost, for the family income. On the other hand, there were already some canny farmers, large and small, who quickly latched on to fresh opportunities to become more efficient, and to make more money.

The drift from the countryside to the urban areas, which had started as a trickle, was well under way by the late 18th century. By then, men and families, in a sometimes desperate search for self-sustainability, had started migrating in increasing numbers to the towns, which, by their very presence, they were to transform. In many instances, they were merely leaving one sort of squalor for another. Increasingly large families meant that the rural population did not go down statistically, but those who stayed knew that some of their most able-bodied members had gone.

William Cobbett, who had worked as a farm labourer as a teenager, was a politician and pamphleteer who angrily took up the cause of the rural poor at this time. In 1830, towards the end of a life frequently at odds with the Establishment, he produced *Rural Rides*, a still highly readable account of rural poverty in the 1820s. It is seen as a definitive work of its kind, even though it is highly subjective and partisan in places.

In the census of 1841, around 70 per cent of the country's population was still adjudged to be primarily agricultural. But that

70 per cent included small-holders, farm workers, cottagers, and servants, as well as paupers and vagrants. Those who had survived the Napoleonic wars and the economic depression which came in its wake remained alongside the new landowners. Some of them were destined to become land-based traders and manufacturers of the new equipment that was ultimately to change the face of farming and put many of the lower orders out of a job. As these companies grew, country-based people were often to form the core of the workforce of such companies. It was the beginning of an important era when rural wealth was not drawn from the land. It is an era unlikely ever to end.

Among those no longer able to work the land, either for themselves or for others, there were those who were driven by adverse circumstances to join the itinerant gangs that were formed to build the country's new road, rail and canal networks. Those taking up such jobs had at least found a means of escaping from the workhouse. These were cheerless places of rigorous discipline and cold comfort which had their origin in the Poor Law Amendment Act of 1834. They separated husbands from wives and both from their children. Even the comforts of beer and tobacco were banned. It was the authorities' explicit intention to make living even more unbearable for the designated "paupers" inside than it was for the wretchedly paid labourers outside. For these, too, were paupers, seeking to subsist on the "outdoor relief" or enduring the stigma of "help from the parish".

The year of the Poor Law amendment was also the year which saw the prosecution of six farm labourers from the Dorset village of Tolpuddle for daring to form a trade union. They were found guilty of conspiring to obstruct the flow of trade and were transported forthwith to Australia. However, widespread protests by sympathisers led to them being granted a pardon two years later. These "martyrs" have been remembered and honoured by trade unionists ever since.

It was not until the early 1870s that there was another brief period of defiance from the grassroots. Once again, a trade union for farm workers was formed. Within an amazingly short time, it was apparent that the union was meeting a real need. Only 12 months after its formation it had nearly 1,000 branches and 72,000 members. The original aim had been to turn "land-tied slaves" into men. But, almost immediately, the new body's sense of direction became distinctly confused as extremists in the membership began pursuing other objectives which were more clearly political. Their arguments were directed against Parliament itself, and even against the Church.

As the union leaders fought to get their new organisation off the ground and to give it the coherence it so badly needed, there came a succession of bad harvests, which in turn led to a growth in food imports. One result of this was that farmers, with a new wind of desperation blowing in their faces, turned against their own men, and some union members grew frustrated at what they saw as the inadequacies of their own union.

Inevitably, the first grouping, the National Agricultural Labourers' Union, suffered as other rival unions were established. By the 1880s, some 700,000 men, women and children had left the land for the cities or for overseas to start a new life. Union membership was to fall to fewer than 5,000.

A Ministry of Agriculture was established in 1889, and the farm workers' lot seemed set once again for an uncertain recovery. But this prospect was almost immediately dashed by a sudden growth in food imports and a dramatic reduction in requirements for home-grown grain. The introduction of refrigeration, for example, meant that American, Australian and New Zealand meat was displacing that produced at home. Farmers and farm workers saw drastic falls in their incomes as the buildings and the infrastructure around them began visibly to decay. Analysts of the late Victorian period have found that "deep and inescapable" poverty afflicted about a third of the wage earning class – in spite of a century of economic advance.

Economic depression, and changes in marketing and distribution practice, led to what one agricultural historian, Victor Bonham-Carter, in a book called *The English Village*, later described as "that long period of economic and social neglect" for English farming. It was effectively to last until the outbreak of the Second World War. For almost half a century, governments showed little interest in increasing domestic food production, or, apart from introducing old age pensions in 1909, in the welfare of the poorest. In the First

World War, the loss of manpower to the trenches was offset by the use of volunteers, soldiers, schoolchildren and women. But after that war, the English countryside was to suffer increasingly from exploitation and neglect.

Almost half a million hectares of the country's best farming land was sold off for development to speculative builders, and the lack of enforceable planning mechanisms meant that new towns and suburbs – half town, half country – encroached upon (often abandoned) green fields. Factories went up on good virgin soil not far from the urban areas, but large tracts of what remained of the rural heritage became a sort of designated playground. The countryside had become a place where people relaxed, not a place where they lived and worked.

Many of the "stalwarts" of village life, wrote Victor Bonham-Carter, were dead or had become ghosts of their former selves. Despite the persistence of nostalgia and the country idyll, it seemed in the encircling political gloom of 1939 that the precious force of English country life was "spent". Inertia, as well as poverty, began stalking the landscape; low wages, for those who were working on the land, became the norm.

It was an unwished-for lull before an unwanted storm. But, ironically, it was the upheavals of the Second World War that were to dispel the gloom of the farmers – and, in some measure, that of the farm labourer. This was a time when the country's economy, like the country itself, found itself under siege. A new regime of subsidies and price controls was introduced, and huge numbers from the Women's Land Army and prisoners of war were drafted in to supplement an eroding labour force.

By the war's end, in 1945, the country was meeting two-thirds of its own food requirements. Two years later, a new Agriculture Act brought in a system of guaranteed prices and a new range of subsidies and grants. It was intended to give a buffeted industry a promise of solvency and a sense of stability which had eluded it for most of the preceding half-century.

For large numbers of less well-off country-dwellers, whose parents had watched aghast as fertile soil, which had provided them with a living, was disposed of by opportunist landowners a quarter of a century before, there were also some life-enhancing developments. For this was also a time when mains electricity, gas and water were extended to rural dwellings over wide areas; the telephone and public transport, as well as car ownership, began to spread. The sense of isolation was not banished, but for many it had become less onerous than it had been only a few years before.

It could have been the dawning of a bright new age for the lower-paid farm workers and others of the rural poor. In fact, they now faced a totally different sort of threat as they found themselves displaced – not by other land workers, but by machines. In the first 20 years after the Second World War, the number of tractors being used in England and Wales more than doubled, from 180,000 to nearly 420,000; the number of combined harvesters leapt from 3,253 to nearly 58,000; the number of milking machines went up from 40,000 to more than 100,000. Most telling, from the intensive labouring point of view, the number of "working" horses on the farm dropped from nearly 440,000 to fewer than 20,000. The gap grew inexorably between well-organised and therefore well-to-do farmers and the much smaller, less wealthy farmers, obliged perhaps to concentrate on stock rearing and grazing.

By the mid-1950s, farming was lucrative – sometimes very lucrative – for the few who owned the bigger holdings. They were earning as much as 20 times more than their poorest colleagues. Even though living standards for most people in farming were improving, the number of unskilled and semi-skilled workers on the land fell steeply. Those at the "low paid" end of the scale were on wages that were markedly lower than those similarly placed in the urban areas.

The acreages of land that were in the hands of the bigger farmers, meanwhile, were to become bigger still. But by 1982, they were employing an average of one full-time worker for every 70 hectares of arable land; a mid-19th century plot of the same extent would need a work force of half a dozen. It became cheaper to remove hedges altogether than to employ someone to maintain them.

Well before this time, it had become apparent that Britain had become an urbanised society, no longer a nation of country-dwellers. As later recessions and the EU's restrictive farm policies began to bite, the situation of the rural deprived and poor, especially where officially vaunted "opportunities" were not readily apparent, became increasingly wretched. For all that, their situation remained one of relative, rather than absolute, poverty.

An answer to the question of what constitutes absolute poverty in rural England today came to me while compiling this book. John Hicks, director of Warwickshire Rural Community Council, was one of several senior community council members, or executives, who responded to a very basic questionnaire I sent to the leaders of all 38 councils in England, asking questions about the nature and evidence of poverty and hardship in their area. "On a regular basis," Hicks replied (in November 1996), "I see human derelicts walking the same highways with their rubbish bags and pushchairs, but I am not in contact with them..."

Such derelicts may be the embodiment of absolute poverty in 20th-century England. But they are not alone. This community may, unwittingly, harbour a recluse; that community may have an extra-ordinary "eccentric" who is living in destitution, but without a clue of the sort of benefits to which he or she may be entitled. But if the John Hickses of this world are not "in contact" with them, who is? Governments which talk of social services and related "safety nets" may be capable of forgetting that a net, by definition, is made of holes – through which the social casualties are liable to slip.

How then, in view of the foregoing, is one to define relative poverty? (It is a question asked in the knowledge that, according to the anti-poverty lobbies, it distracts attention from what should be done about the problems it throws up!) The history of the last two centuries has provided a mass of contributory circumstantial evidence as to how the poor became poor, but their "condition" in the late 20th century remains an area of only intermittent political argument.

A decade and a half before the Copenhagen meeting, while discussing poverty in Britain, Peter Townsend, writing in 1979, suggested: "Individuals can be said to be in poverty when they lack the resources to obtain the types of diet, participate in the activities and have the living conditions and amenities which are customary, or at least widely encouraged and approved, in the societies to which they belong." This definition appeared in the same year that Margaret Thatcher led the Conservatives into power. Her arrival was accompanied by some pre-arranged, portentous and quasi-egalitarian quotations from St Francis of Assissi that she read from a slip of paper as she stood on the threshold of 10 Downing Street. These words, of all the words she could have chosen, were to usher Britain into an era which brought dramatic increases in the numbers of the poor. It was also to see an erosion of those often politically motivated but ostensibly caring organisations – such as the trade unions – that could have been so active at grassroots level on the poor's behalf.

The Townsend definition is one which has been broadly accepted and much used by specialists in the field ever since. It can be readily applied to a way of life which is familiar enough to many hundreds of thousands of households in the English countryside. It is an existence which is lived out in an environment where total privacy can be hard to come by, where life may be conducted "in a goldfish bowl", because too many other people know more than enough about each other's circumstances. It is a life which also has positive aspects, but, in the words of one resident of the Derbyshire Peak District, "there is nowhere to hide in the countryside". More precise definitions of poverty may be elusive, but the symptoms, in town as well as country, are many and varied and they are readily identifiable. The CPAG has suggested, in its own down-to-earth way, that poverty in the 1990s is not only about social exclusion imposed by an inadequate income and going short of food or clothing; it is also about lacking the means to join the local sports club, to send children on the school trip which all the others are joining, or to go out with friends because one cannot, in one way or another, keep up.

"I hated Chistmas," said one mother questioned by Elaine Kempson in 1994. "I would have preferred it for people not to give me anything because I wouldn't have felt obliged to give back. I found it very hard ... like in November, if I found I had a pound or two spare I would put it in a jar ... I gave them all some little thing each, but you feel like it is nothing."

Poverty in England in the 1990s is, as it has always been, about doing without necessities. Adam Smith, writing in the late 18th century (*Wealth of Nations*), said that "necessities" were not only those things which are indispensably necessary for the support of life, but also "whatever the custom of the country renders it indecent for creditable people, even of the lowest order, to be without". It took nearly two generations after these words appeared for the beginnings of poverty relief and procedures to be set in place by which unacceptably low wages could be supplemented by the parish.

But these beginnings were not deemed adequate by militants who became active on behalf of the rural disadvantaged. They were desperate men, desperate enough to instigate riots in the countryside as

> *In Buckinghamshire:*
> **"Most services are conspicuously missing! Some villages have no services and no transport to get them to centralised services. Low expectations are a real issue... (but) they don't make a fuss, campaign, etc, when the services go or when they don't have access to them."**

well as the towns, physically attacking and abusing rural parish dignitaries and wrecking agricultural machinery, maiming livestock, and turning to poaching as a way of life. Today's rural poverty is a less visible, more private affair and it has called for desperate measures of a different order. All too often, because it is suppressed and hidden, it can lead to mental health problems, to clinical depression and even, statistically speaking, a high rate of suicide.

Peter Townsend returned to his theme in 1996, this time on the eve of the day when many expected the Conservative Party to be voted out of power. In a book called *A Poor Future*, he warned that "the UK is skidding even faster than other countries down the slippery slope of increasing poverty and inequality". The consequences, he suggested, of poverty getting more extensive while the prosperity of the rich was continuing to grow substantially would be "levels of social instability which will be difficult for all but the most ruthless and authoritarian governments to control". This was the tip of an iceberg in the concern that was being less and less surreptitiously voiced by a small but growing band of opinion formers. These were the individuals who pointed to the incidence of violence and crime, and the fear of such things, that were creeping up on and disturbing community life – particularly, but not only, in the inner cities.

Cassandras and empiricists among the ranks of practising sociologists and newspaper columnists were joined by a motley collection of television progamme makers, novelists and playwrights who were beginning to depict such aspects of late 20th century living with a wearying predictability.

From some people in rural areas, there came what might be called the predictable, hardy perennial response. Such depictions, they maintained, may be applicable to the inner city, but they have little to do with the English countryside. People in power in the goldfish-bowl communities would perhaps add that they or "the neighbours" would be quickly aware of any discord rippling the social surface, just as they would know of any "real" deprivation on their doorsteps. And they would say that there were always elements in their communities – including perhaps the more discreet leaders of those communities, as well as the extended families of those who were suffering – who would be available to some how nip the unaceptable in the bud or to help out those who were in difficult circumstances.

The presiding heads of the Women's Institute in a small village in rural Wiltshire, when they were questioned in the summer of 1995 by researchers led by Paul Milbourne, of the Countryside Unit, based in Cheltenham College of Further Education, announced that they would very quickly be aware of any deprivation in their village. Anyway, they added, Pewsey village "didn't have a lot of problems".

This sort of argument has validity in certain contexts, and works well enough in some Third World societies. In contemporary England, however, it can be delivered with a pursed smile, and can carry more than a whiff of that one-eye-closed Victorian philanthropism. Country people, like people anywhere else, have their pride, even in the most adverse circumstances, and – especially in a goldfish bowl – they will keep their poverty and the accompanying hardships to themselves.

Whether it is out of pride, shyness or obstinacy, such individuals will refuse to admit they are suffering. Some members of their peer group may, of course, be able and willing to articulate their troubles. They will talk openly of dependence on Social Security payments or of low wages, overcrowding and other sorts of deprivation. But for an incalculable number, self-respect can also dictate that they remain determined to keep the evidence of their hardship hidden.

In nine cases out of 10, people on low incomes are not the stuff of which martyrs are made, even though the stigma and the shame of poverty in a small or scattered community can be very hard to carry. The "poor", after all, may not always be recognisable. But their ability to keep their poverty hidden, for whatever reason, can lead to some of them finding themselves, and feeling very strongly, marginalised or powerless — something which may be, just occasionally, of their own making.

Causes of rural poverty in England today vary as widely as the landscapes in which it is found: one deprived area of England can be totally unlike another less than an hour's journey away.

In the heart of Kent, which the idyll-mongers like to call the Garden of England, for instance, there are former coal-mining communities living only a 10-minute drive from the heart of the cathedral city of Canterbury. Here, there is unemployment running at more than 30 per cent and I have met men still in their 30s or 40s – some of them former miners who once earned "decent" wages – who have been deleted from the unemployment register to take temporary jobs on a local building site at £10 a week on top of State benefits.

The £10 these men receive is the current upper limit of what they can earn without their benefits being cut. A Rowntree Foundation report in May 1997, urged that the £10 figure should be increased to £30 a week, saying that the unemployed should be better rewarded for trying to help themselves and not "shackled to poverty", as under the existing laws. In the following months, pressures to increase the £10 figure intensified.

The men of Kent referred to above were engaged under a short-term partnership scheme with a local college and found themselves in a situation where their self-respect was sorely tried. When I asked them what they thought of the scheme, they suggested with undisguised contempt that the Prime Minister, or perhaps his deputy, should put on a hard hat and see how they got on.

Not many miles from Stonehenge, one of the most visited landmarks on the tourist itinerary of England, and within half an hour's drive of the Cotswolds, there are a number of villages adjoining the former bases of units of the RAF and the Army. The original raison d'être of these villages has been seriously undermined, and in some cases has disappeared altogether, as a result of the so-called peace dividend. Some of them are not so many miles away from "problem-free" Pewsey, though the lifestyles of the local inhabitants seem far removed. Jobs which were in defence or in related industries have been wound down which means that the economy of whole villages has been badly hit.

"A number of families are in debt," a social worker employed in this area told Paul Milbourne during his researches. "Their poverty amazes me... I'm saying they are poor – things like they can't afford to send their children to playgroup, or the family live on baked beans on toast for the second half of the month... I have mothers coming in to ask for spare nappies because they can't afford to buy any more – things like that."

In the predominantly and more traditionally agricultural areas of East Anglia and Lincolnshire, wages on the land have always been notoriously low. Nevertheless, a farm job, even though it is seasonal and the work conditions may be appalling, is often the only work available. In some areas, even the lowest wages are undercut by the (illegal) use of child labour or "gangs" of the unemployed who are bussed in for what could be called clandestine exploitation. These are people who come from the recesses of the deprived inner cities of Sheffield, Birmingham or some other metropolitan centre. A further complication is that many of them are members of ethnic minorities who may barely understand the exploitation to which they are submitting themselves.

But there is another side to this coin. The farmers themselves, even if they do not own the huge holdings referred to above, may be operating on the narrowest of margins, or no margins at all. They belong to a profession which once was the backbone of the country-side and one of the country's most successful businesses, but in which, today, everything has changed. Large-scale agri-business, which has produced what some analysts describe as "industrial sites in rural locations", has prospered during the 1990s. But it has been at the expense of many displaced small farmers, and those who remain of this dwindling band may well find that success for them is an elusive commodity. Farmers in 1990s Britain, and their wives, have perceptibly been moving up the list of individuals who have found themselves in need of stress counselling. They are a species which has been washed over repeatedly by tides of unfamiliar, and therefore unwelcome, British and European Union legislation and so were already on the list even before the great and prolonged BSE crisis began (in the late 1980s) to eat into profits and, in the mid-1990s, when there were reports that the bottom had fallen out of the potato market. Poverty in the countryside is as real as a plate of chips.

The farm workers know as well as anyone that the heyday of farming in Britain has long since past. The "treats" to which farm workers were – and felt – entitled only a generation or two ago – such as a bumper supper to celebrate a bumper harvest – are now a rarity. Before the industrial revolution, agriculture was the biggest industry in Britain and the biggest employer, providing close to half the national income. It now employs less than two out of every 100 people living in the countryside. The largest farms are often managed on behalf of big commercial companies or distant landowners, and half the country's farmers are part-timers.

The compilers of the RDC's 1994 *Lifestyles* report stated that non-agricultural employment accounted in some areas for as much as 95 per cent of the work force, and never for less than 75 per cent. Employment and the ability to find it were regarded as "very important" components of people's willingness to live in the country, and well over half those surveyed, in several counties, declared that they found difficulties in getting a job. Many of them said the fact that they lived in the countryside presented very specific disadvantages in their search for a job.

Not surprisingly, the same survey threw up evidence of what the compilers described as a "vigorous" informal job market. Clearly, enforcement of the law in the matter of employment can be difficult in underpopulated rural areas, and employers may see themselves as only human if they seek to get away with what they can get away with. On the other hand, as seasonal fruit and vegetable pickers in the Lincolnshire Fens and in Leicestershire have testified, the inadequately supervised working conditions can be appalling as well as illegal.

Without the sort of all-embracing supervision that it is impossible to introduce, the hidden economy will remain an unignorable, but also not inconsiderable, component of countryside life. Second jobs and casual work, even where they blur into illegality, are more than just a significant area of activity; where there is intolerable hardship, they can become the norm. For so long as the number of single parents remains high in the countryside, the proportion of women doing part-time jobs will also continue to have a very measurable impact on local economies and social structures.

Ironically, it is just this proliferation of part-time jobs which, to the passing visitor, may give the impression of economic buoyancy in the countryside. A weekend visit to this or that souvenir shop, pub, tea-room or fruit farm, or an overnight stay in an attractive hotel or bed and breakfast establishment, yields little more than a glimpse of a situation which is coincidentally illegal and fundamentally exploitative.

The school-age teenager waiting at the meal table or serving behind the bar, the child helping to unload a delivery lorry, the woman washing up in the back kitchen, the pensioner sorting produce, away from the counter, in the farm shop may all be there quite willingly, grateful for the distraction, as well as the money, the job may bring. But the very slim nature of the pay packet they are getting for the tasks they perform would probably astonish the well-meaning visitor.

In a number of penetrating research studies of rural poverty, commissioned in the mid-1980s but for some reason unpublished by the authorities who commissioned them (though still relevant and invaluable to researchers today), Brian McLaughlin sought, with a fresh array of revealing statistics, to disentangle the reality from the rhetoric (his words) of rural disadvantage. The full extent of the rural poor's marginalisation, he wrote, is underlined by the patterns of inequality in the distribution of household income. It is wages that determine status – and low wages mean, more often than not, low status.

The poorest of the poor in the countryside tend to be the elderly, and especially the elderly living alone. But where measurable poverty may be determined by income, deprivation and disadvantage are determined by other factors. The old, the disabled, the sick and the representatives of ethnic minorities who live in rural areas know at least as surely as their urban brothers and sisters the nature of their deprivation. To be homeless or in debt in the countryside can be at least as disconcerting, and the cause of just as much depression, as in the town or inner city.

People in such circumstances, if they have lived in the locality for a number of years, may be susceptible to an otherwise commendable pride at their show of apparent independence. On the other hand, they may be susceptible to a certain sense of resignation, a lethargy almost, which places them in the category of the marginalised and the powerless. "Poverty," in the words of Carey Oppenheim in 1993, "impinges on relationships with others and yourself... It stops people being able to take control of their own lives." "Poverty," says ACRE, "is as real in rural areas as in urban areas, but rural poverty is different in its depth, colour and dynamics." In the pages that follow, the nature of that differentness will be explored.

The arguments may do little to dint the chocolate-box image of the countryside which can be so reassuring to the wistful nostalgist, pleasing to the urban escapist, and soothing to the many who seek it out when they are under stress. But statistically-backed facts indicate that, according to widely accepted criteria, as many as one in four country-dwellers may be living in or near the margins of poverty. And they can't eat the scenery.

Chapter *three*

Grounds for Protest

*This landscape of open skies and smooth-rounded peaks
still has a lightness to lift the spirits. But for those
choosing to strike out along one of the myriad droves or
trackways there is no such refreshment for the soul. This
is no living tapestry. It is a landscape of the dead. The
most striking feature is the silence....*

Graham Harvey,
The Killing of the Countryside, London, 1997

how precious is the rural idyll? It has been around for centuries, but its latest manifestations may be said to have been enshrined in 1949. The Act of that year led to the setting up of the country's National Parks. They were not universally popular, not least because they were perceived as coming into being to meet the needs of city-dwellers. But it has been partly out of these same needs that a proliferation of protests, often orchestrated from an urban setting, have grown on behalf of the English countryside.

The protesters come in all shapes and sizes. Their activities in many cases have had the effect, which some may deplore, of helping to rationalise and to preserve the idyll. In social terms, their activities have been fascinating. But in more hard-nosed economic terms, where investment has been at stake, there have been moments when they have been less than welcome.

At their most extreme, these people have been easy to stereotype. In quality newspapers, they have come across often as people who, regardless of their political convictions in the normal sense, have made a "thing" out of protest. They turn up at an agreed rallying point to add their weight and a touch of class to a very 20th-century sort of struggle. Their objection has been to a new motorway or by-pass, perhaps, or against another hypermarket.

Some may turn up in their Range Rover or its European or Japanese equivalent – or, if they are discreet, they may have left it at home. In their readiness for a good scrap, they may have donned their green wellies and matching anoraks. Like the struggles in which they participate, they are themselves a late 20th-century phenomenon.

At the other extreme, some of the activists have been portrayed as engaging, but possibly half-witted, folk-heroes. These are the ones for whom the adjective "weird" may be most appropriate. They may have a penchant for living in ad hoc tree "houses" or for driving tunnels beneath this or that development site. All these and many more represent a steadily growing grassroots energy that has yet to be harnessed – though that fact is, of course, contributory to their strength.

These protesters have been able to chalk up some remarkable successes. In the countryside, they have given power to the elbows of some of the rurally-based lobbies with whom they automatically sympathise. These lobbies tacitly sympathise with them, often when they may be precluded by charitable rules from joining in such explicitly political activities.

In the rural context, the protest – or the more down-market "demo" – has become a device by which articulate representatives of the educated and better-off middle class have been able to make political waves, as well as headlines. One former Minister of Transport announced within a couple of years of resigning from the government benches that protesters against one of his motorway schemes had been right all along. It has been a sign of the times that some of the self-proclaimed Friends of the Earth or members of the Green Party have stood for the local council, or for Parliament, and even in urban areas have occasionally won a seat or two on their local council.

It is usually the allegedly arbitrary nature of planning decisions affecting the rural areas that has brought out the dissenters. John Ruskin may be counted a forerunner. In Victoria's time, he delivered himself of sombre moral and social judgments in all sorts of areas. One of these was in protest at what he saw as the destructive impact of the arrival of the railway in rural beauty spots. He was appalled, for instance, that the steam engines should be allowed to intrude and bring train-loads of undesirables to Monsal Dale, one of the most peaceful corners of Derbyshire.

On one wall of the viaduct which crosses that dale there is a plaque which recalls the words he spoke – though only on behalf of a small and relatively privileged minority. Somewhat piquantly, in the late 1990s, in the wake of the all-embracing privatisation of Britain's railways, controversial moves were afoot to reinstate the railway back along the same lines, to the very same spot in Monsal Dale. If they show signs of bearing any fruit, it will be astonishing if latter-day John Ruskins do not emerge to warn, once again, against destruction of the prevailing idyll.

When work started on a by-pass to take traffic round the Berkshire town of Newbury in the mid-1990s, representatives of the "objecting classes" were quickly up in arms. This was Home Counties Berkshire, after all. As usual, they came from across the social board to pitch into melées in the mud; and, once again, their infinite variety was not untypical of the age.

There were children in pushchairs, accompanied by fighting Mums. These, in some cases, were the wives or partners of locally-resident celebrities. In some cases, too, they were celebrities in their own right – usually as a result of accomplishments in London or some nearby urban setting. There were protesters from the professional classes, others who were shiftless and/or unemployed, and still others who came along for "a bit of a lark" or because they had a day off from their routine job.

There was even an element of fun about participating – tree houses, rope bridges and so on belong in part, at least, to some childhoods. But, even so, a large proportion were in dead earnest. Some were educated enough to be able to explain their views at some length, even to the extent of drawing up skilfully devised alternative plans for the projected trunk road or whatever. It became apparent in this period that the roots of protest could sprout as easily in working class soil as they would in richer soil.

Although, in the process of achieving what many of them counted as resounding successes, they made headlines and became very visible on television news screens, such people did not always sweep all before them. Governments, and the thick-skinned, government-backed contractors who had been taken on to carry out such huge civil engineering jobs, mounted very sophisticated counter-operations to crush protesters' activities. Ironically, this often meant recruiting casual labour from the same social groups (educated, unemployed, educated unemployed, and so on) as those making up the opposition.

A colleague at *The Guardian*, John Vidal, vigorously iconoclastic by nature but usually fair-minded in his writings against the Newbury by-pass (and on the environment generally), managed to get taken on – no questions asked – as a security guard. The working conditions that he encountered, as he later reported, were disgusting. Morale among these troops, he found, was almost non-existent – "it was a job, after all", they said – but he and they had to take orders to beat back, sometimes physically, the very protesters his articles supported.

As his referee on the application form for the job, John had given the name of one Michael Howard, of Eastbourne. He had been Environment Secretary and later Home Secretary. John agreed that he learned much in this exercise, and later in the tunnels that were built by protesters close to Manchester Airport, about the significance of the rural idyll in the British psyche. The protesters, after all, were by and large the very people who were responsible nowadays for keeping the idyll in existence. But he also learned much about the methods employed by contracting companies for whom this same idyll was hardly a priority concept.

The activities of these protesters, and the developers in their way, are directly relevant to the thrust of this book because they have given much conscious or unconscious satisfaction to the idyll-mongers. Many of the late 20th century's protesters have operated unthinkingly (perhaps) according to the oft-repeated mantras of the Countryside Commission where the main purpose of life is "to keep the countryside beautiful". Where the protesters' moves have been backed by arguments for sensible preservation or conservation, they have been able to win votes. The former minister who spoke up on their behalf became, for a brief period anyway, something of a good guy.

But contrast the relative successes of such protesters with the less conspicuous achievements of those who agitate to achieve a better deal for the marginalised and powerless poor. However worthy and honourable the ideas that motivate them, these individuals can expect, almost before they launch any serious protest activity, that there will be attempts to elbow them out of sight.

In Lincolnshire:

"Evidence of poverty can be seen in people's clothing, and to some extent their demeanour, but you have to know what you are looking for. People do not talk about it explicitly (with the exception of some young people), but accept it often with a degree of resignation."

These people do not tend to win votes, as the Greens and Friends of the Earth may win votes. It is a peculiarly English fact that a movement which seeks to pull down the unsightly old pithead winding gear at a defunct colliery in, say, County Durham or Nottinghamshire, or a movement to preserve it at all costs if it is suddenly deemed worthy of "listing", will cause more of a stir than a movement by a handful of individuals who want to get mains electricity and water installed for families living in two or three wretched old houses up on the nearby hillside.

In a caring society, the political exchanges which preceded the 1997 election could have been of far-reaching social significance. It fell to the politically sensitive Church of England, in its own report on the plight of the unemployed, to cause more of a stir in this area. But even this was a stir which did not last much longer than 24 hours.

The poor were not ignored entirely, but often they became more a side-line rather than the central point of the argument. It now remains to be seen whether poverty will become a "real" issue under a new government, or whether it will remain a matter of acute concern only to the poor themselves and the minority groups who campaign on their behalf.

Propositions that Britain had become a polarised, and therefore unfair and unjust, society during the 1970s and 1980s broke some ice, but the pond generally remained frozen. When out-going Conservative ministers, including the Prime Minister himself, announced he cared about the have-nots because he had once been one himself, the ring of plausibility was hollow. It would have been enough to provoke a wry smile on the face of Francis of Assissi, the saint whose name and whose cause had been famously and fraudulently invoked by John Major's predecessor, Margaret Thatcher.

However, there have been some very substantial items on the political agenda of the mid-1990s which have impinged, directly, on the poor. The condition and the availability of the National Health Service, the state of the education system, and the "successes" of a streamlined, distinctly lean economy, have become the bread-and-butter issues of knockabout party politics. But knockabouts are not serious political debates: these debates are still to come.

Because the poor have rarely in history actually won votes, they could not be attractive raw material for the confrontations of the hustings. By the same token, the international "year" for the eradication of poverty, which was solemnly launched during 1996 under United Nations auspices, made little impact on public consciousness even though its lease of life was in fact extended beyond the original twelve months. The true nature of poverty in England today, whether in town or country, may still lead some to drugs or drink or into some forms of anti-social behaviour, but it has not, if we are honest, kept many of us awake at nights – except, of course, the poor themselves.

But where the nature of the public political debate may have provided platforms for only muted protests on behalf of the rural poor and the deprived, there have been intermittent moments of real concern. These have been in the meeting rooms of civil servants and of one-off committees set up to consider their findings, rooms which have sometimes echoed very audibly to strains of heartening disagreement. Sparks have been known to fly when a representative of this or that concerned voluntary sector pressure group, usually in the shape of a well-informed adviser, has stepped into the presence of such civil servants, or even parliamentary select committees.

On some occasions, this has has been a case of the obdurate confronting the immovable. On other occasions, it has been the enthusiast looking into the ill-focused eyes of the world-weary legislator. But on more fruitful occasions, it has provided an opportunity for the enlightened to engage in a head-to-head with the uninformed.

A fraught subject of confrontation, so far as the countryside is concerned, is what has come to be called the "sparsity factor". This relates to that proportion of centrally authorised resources which may or may not be allocated to meet the special needs of rural areas. The fraughtness arises when one looks closely at the small print of the budgets for public services, such as education, transport or community health care, comparing what resources are being made available for the urban areas with what is meant for rural areas in general and for "very rural" areas in particular. These are the ones where the population may be widely scattered across a landscape which may be inhospitable at the best of times and probably impassable in winter.

The sparsity factor has thrown up its own ammunition for those engaged in political confrontation. They have launched a debate from a starting point which says that meeting the needs of three households in the remoter parts of the Yorkshire Dales, for example, is much more complicated logistically – and financially – than meeting the needs of three similarly placed households all in the same street in inner-city Sheffield or Leeds.

In the Spring of 1996, the Rural Development Commission, to vociferous support from ACRE and other concerned organisations, published its own commissioned assessment of the criteria used when centrally allocated resources were being determined in Whitehall. It was, in fact, more of a critique than an assessment. To what extent, it asked, were these criteria meeting the specific requirements of supposed end-users?

The assessment scrutinised closely the methods used by government to determine the amount of funds intended to support local authority health, housing and social services. Their findings strongly reinforced the view that the mechanisms and criteria employed by government, based as they often were on experience in deprived urban areas, implicitly failed to appreciate the special requirements of people living in the countryside. The subject of central resource allocations will come up a number of times in these pages, and discrepancies will be highlighted in the fields of health and housing.

Standard Spending Assessments (SSAs) is the name given by government to the increasingly controversial instrument it uses to determine the amount of funding per head that should be allocated from central sources to top up local funds being made available to the statutory providers of services, including local authorities. It is an amount which is reappraised each year and which, each year, produces howls of anguish from those authorities feeling the pinch. When the researcher, Rita Hale, placed the figures for 1995-96 under her microscope she concentrated on discrepancies between the provision for rural areas and the provision for metropolitan areas and inner London boroughs. Her findings were followed by gestures of consternation in many quarters.

The SSAs for local authority services in that year averaged £648 for each person living in the predominantly rural shire counties, against £756 for his or her cousin in the metropolitan city, £798 for a metaphorically more distant relation in an outer London borough, and all of £1,154 for someone living in the other world of an inner London borough. But SSAs, the researchers found, were being determined in Whitehall by civil servants who were working on the basis of population size, with population sparsity given little weight. This meant inner London boroughs were being authorised to spend – and were therefore allocated – about £1.78 per person, against £1 per person being allocated to councils in the rural shires to provide the same range of services.

The Whitehall response, as far it goes, is that a sparsity weighting of £16 a head is in fact added to the shire county allocation of £648. To this, the assessors respond, the £16 is not being adduced with any consistency. While there may be a top-up for education, there is none for personal social services.

Whitehall then wades in with a rejoinder that it measures carefully the numbers of lone parents, ethnic minorities and those living in overcrowded housing conditions, to which the assessors come back with the charge that almost no account is taken of the necessarily higher costs – in terms of time, manpower, vehicle wear-and-tear, or buildings maintenance, or in service delivery — in the countryside.

Economies of scale are difficult enough to accomplish, let alone capitalise on, in the rural areas. They simply don't apply.

Similar arguments have been conducted with some intensity inside the Department of Health. It too provides what it sees as target allocations for spending by local District Health Authorities (DHAs) on local hospitals, and on community and family health service facilities. But once again, according to the rural lobby, resources are being allocated more according to size of population, adjusted to meet supposed local needs and costs as well as (in this context) age.

The result is another victory for the urban providers. DHAs in the towns and cities are inevitably better off, in terms of resources per head, than their counterparts in rural areas. In inner London, the allocation to Camden and Islington DHA came to £627 per person in 1995-96. This is more than 60 per cent higher than that for the most sparsely populated DHA, Cambridge and Huntingdon, which got £389. The difference persists in spite of the fact that in rural areas like Cambridge and Huntingdon, old people living alone, or single parents who are ill or giving birth, may be obliged to stay longer in hospital when there are fewer support services for them at home. Further variations on the health theme, and the inconsistencies to which they give rise, will be discussed in a later chapter.

Generally speaking in the "sparsity" context, it is the wider view that seems most obviously to be missing. One astonishing reason for this is that there seems to be no universally satisfactory body of data of real need in country areas which is simultaneously available for scrutiny by all interested parties and also updated on a regular basis.

Grist to the mill of this debate, meanwhile, comes from the National Council for Voluntary Organisations (NCVO). In its own venture into auditing the publicly available figures, Jenny Gould argues that a lot of information on urban deprivation can be gleaned from a close scanning of the national census. However, the same cannot be said for the rural areas, where there is no agreed system for collecting information on the impact of the sparsity factor in the provision of services. A co-ordinated appraisal of work done by individual local authorities would clearly be a sensible starting point if only the officials concerned were willing, in the words of one of them, to "pull together".

Housing is another acutely sensitive issue which will be discussed in more detail in later pages. While the Housing Corporation, the Government's appointed funding distribution agency for "social" housing, does make special allowances for rural areas from its own constantly diminishing kitty, it too tends to use urban indicators when determining the amounts of money that will be advanced to favoured local councils and housing associations. Rural factors, such as the rise in house prices as a result of inward migration of those with money (and the understandable greed, it should be added, of country folk who follow the market and demand high prices when they have to sell), and the need for affordable and specifically local housing for rent, tend generally not to get the close attention that is essential in such a unique set of circumstances.

In the White Paper on rural affairs which the Government published in 1995, the chosen theme was that there should be what it called a "living" countryside. (In the space of only a few years, it seems, the "living" countryside has become very much a living cliche.) Ministers were clearly pleased with the mini-historic step they said they had taken, but as soon as the White Paper was published the awkward questions started to fly.

Where, it was asked, should the official line be drawn between "living" at what presumably would be agreed was an acceptable standard of living and surviving at an unacceptable level of deprivation? Certainly, no clear line was visible in the White Paper itself, nor was there any hint that one might officially exist.

The authorised Whitehall view of levels of social and economic development and consequential need can be gauged approximately from data published by the Department of the Environment in what it calls the Index of Local Conditions (1994). This data, however, is only minimally satisfactory, since in several areas it is out of date even before it is printed. In recent years, this has been partly as a result of administrative boundary changes along lines proposed only a short time before by the Local Government Commission.

Once again, the almost reflex response to the material has been one of impatience. ACRE, among others, has argued that it is fundamentally flawed, for the simple reason that the criteria used have taken on irreconcilably different meanings in different contexts.

Thus, high car ownership in an urban environment can indicate a measure of affluence, while in the countryside, where public services may be distinctly scanty, it may well reflect an imperative need to have one's own transport. Indeed, having one's own vehicle in the countryside can exacerbate poverty, since maintaining one on a low income can be unpredictably expensive. A car shared, in most instances, is by definition a car that is available to only one party at a time – a direct cause of tension perhaps, and, in its own way, an indirect cause of unwished-for isolation.

Looking at jobs, the same Index of Local Conditions uses educational qualifications and registered employment figures as yardsticks. However, high academic qualifications in the countryside do not necessarily enhance local job prospects, and certainly do not ensure high wages. (Nor, in 1990s Britain, do they guarantee such things in the town – but that is another story.) Research has shown that sophisticated manufacturers who choose to move from an urban to a rural location often bring their workforce with them. Such manufacturers, it transpires, have made their move – sometimes with financial incentives from central or local government – in the expectation that company overheads will be cheaper in the countryside and that surroundings will be more congenial and less stressful for members of the workforce and their families. It is nothing like so simple and things are not what they seem.

The fallibility of methods generally used by government departments and their auditors to collate data on wealth and income can be ascertained very quickly. Averages that have been postulated for the rural context can be seriously misleading. Thus, a modern village of only a few hundred, whether it is in Cumbria or Cornwall, may have a third of the population earning £40,000 a year, while another third – if they are in work – may be earning less than £6,000.

"This just goes to show," says ACRE and those who support its views, by way of comment on such figures, "that the picture has simply got to be more complete. Rural people are not asking for special treatment. They are asking only for fair treatment."

Chapter *four*
What is 'Poor'?

There aren't many opportunities for them to have a laugh. There's a need for them to have a laugh, and that's missing. Life is very serious in Tidworth... I get very cross when people say, "Look, they can't afford to send their child to playgroup and they're smoking." Well, for some of them, that's all they have...

Wiltshire social worker, 1993

We have to settle for enough to live on... There's no hand-outs, and we wouldn't lower ourselves to ask a neighbour to help us out. I would like to think I could offer my children opportunities that I have had, but I don't see it...

Carl, Peak District farm worker

Some days we do run out of money. We feed the children first, but my wife and I do sometimes go without, or make do with a sandwich.

Mick, family man in his 30s, Peak District

the first of these quotes is from an agency person working with people in the former Army village of Tidworth in the Kennet district of Wiltshire in 1993-94. The second and third emerged in conversations during research made at about the same time by representatives of the Peak District Rural Deprivation Forum.

Paul Milbourne, who led the Wiltshire research, says exclusion and isolation were the words most often used by residents and agency workers whom he met there. However, although most of his respondents were keen to see improvements in the economic well-being of their immediate area, many also felt disillusioned, dejected and disempowered by their situation. They were generally sceptical that local agencies could achieve much on their behalf, and they were resigned to a fate they couldn't begin to describe.

Wiltshire, like predominantly rural parts of North Yorkshire, Derbyshire, Nottinghamshire and many of the coastal districts of England, has seen its heavy industries decline in the 1980s. The once huge coal industry, which had employed tens of thousands of men and women and which shaped an industrial revolution and, with it, a series of unique societies, has almost disappeared, along with a host of ancillary service industries. A whole way of life – rural as well as urban, since so many pits were in country areas – was deleted with the stroke of a ministerial pen.

The deletion was seen by many as explicitly political, coming as it did in the wake of a deeply controversial miners' strike, but ministers maintained it was because the decision had been made to produce power by markedly cheaper alternative fuels. This strike, it should not be forgotten, was in many senses a rural event. It led to bitterness and anger and divided many families – those for and those against prolonging the action – and in several cases led to the disintegration of rural communities. Wounds sustained at the time have not all healed.

All that remains now of the coal industry, and the spin-off businesses that depended upon it, are a handful of deep mines and a few highly profitable pockets of open-cast mining in the hands of a small number of private developers and speculators. In many instances, the brass bands have stopped playing, the annual galas and street or village parties are no longer held, communities and families have dis-integrated, and once-proud men, as many as one in four of them on the dole, have become alcoholics or drug abusers. Hundreds of small communities, each of them embracing what was once a very vivid set of social and cultural values, have vanished.

At the same time, there have been the ramifications of the "peace dividend". This positive-sounding phrase came into currency as a consequence of the collapse of Soviet power and the Warsaw Pact. It led to the burial of notions of cold war confrontation, but it also led to the disbanding of several military units in the West Country and the North of England and to the loss of thousands of associated jobs. Once again, an important part of the fabric of British society – like it or not – has virtually disappeared.

Nor is that all. Britain's entry into the post-industrial age has been signalled by the running down or the closure of many large-scale heavy manufacturing and engineering plants. There has even been a sharp fall in North Sea fish supplies, caused in part by the excessive plundering of the stock by vessels, British and foreign, whose crews have chosen to ignore EU directives. This has inevitably led to a dramatic and highly disputatious streamlining of the British fishing industry. The idyll of fishermen on the quayside – thickly accented wise old men in grey sweaters, puffing away at big-bowled pipes of tobacco – may still exist on seaside post-cards, but has in fact almost completely disappeared.

The consequence is not just that life has been turned upside down for people who live, and earned their living, in cities and towns which once throbbed with locally-generated econom-ic activity. It is also that these urban centres, which were so important as providers of employment and recreation for surrounding villages and com-munities, have ceased to have

> In Norfolk:
> **"There might be feelings of shame involved in being poor, and some frustra-tion, but this is accepted philosophically."**

the same meaning. Many have become ghost communities, wind tunnels echoing, if they echo at all, to the sounds of ephemeral popular music.

Obviously, there are still pockets of prosperity and there is plenty of activity. Large numbers of "new" entrepreneurs, most notably in the service industries, have made small fortunes, and others will do the same. But many urban street markets have lost their former significance and been run down, to be replaced by out-of-town shopping centres. It is these centres that now draw in the surrounding population, rather as the old street markets used to do. But the hypermarkets and the large department stores do not have the same one-to-one intimacy or the raucous friendliness that their forebears brought to the business of buying and selling.

In May 1997, a modestly-funded national organisation, Action for Market Towns, was launched by the Rural Development Commission. The new body defined small market towns as having populations of less than 15,000 – of which there are nearly 900 in England – and said the need for the new body arose as a result of job losses, the growth of out-of-town shopping centres, as well as crime and the loss of community spirit engendered by empty properties and vandalism. It was, the RDC announced, a chance for the affected towns "to fight back". It was also, though the RDC did not say this, an admission of mistakes in some of the planning policies of the preceding few years.

The traditional role of urban centres as providers of escapist entertainment, on the other hand, has been much enhanced. New-style music clubs, raves and other centres have now become the magnets for bored young people from the countryside catchment areas. The availability of alcohol and drugs, as well as the companionship of a wider and livelier peer group, have produced an enticing sense of freedom that is elusive in a rural setting.

In early 1997, the RDC published its own study of how employment patterns have changed in the Rural Development Areas. These areas were designated by the Government three years earlier, covering a rural population of 3 million people who were contending ("in theory", said the RDC) with "the worst social and economic problems".

The report contained a series of mixed messages. One was that the overall number of jobs in the areas had gone up by just under 120,000 in the 10 years to 1991. Another was that this tally of jobs was in fact offset by the increase in the size of the working population and the proportion of women who were looking for work. Jobs had fallen dramatically in farming and mining but had grown in the service sector.

This meant the authors could announce that while unemployment in most RDAs was below the national average, in five of them (Durham, North-east Derbyshire, Nottinghamshire, Cleveland and Doncaster) it was more than 20 per cent of the male workforce. Some had "retired" early, some (understandably) were registered long-term sick, and some were said to be not actively seeking work. These were often people who were discouraged by the fact that job opportunities, as the report put it, were "limited".

A closer reading of the report yielded a number of blemishes in the only intermittently rosy picture. Despite an overall natural increase of 20,000 in the male workforce in the 10-year period, the number of men without jobs had gone up by nearly twice that figure. With women, the increase had been just under 16,000, but the workforce had gone up by almost 80,000. More than 55 per cent of the total workforce of the RDAs are now employed in the service industries – that is, doing jobs which are predominantly seasonal in character, and therefore insecure and low paid. Tellingly, the report did not touch on incomes, and had nothing to say on the trauma involved in the wholesale changes to a familiar way of life.

Thus, it was the Church, in April 1997, which put a finger on the human – as opposed to the political – realities of unemployment. Children, it warned, were growing up in communities where regular work had been unknown for a generation or more, and they were learning to accept unemployment as a way of life. "We seem," wrote the Rev. David Sheppard, Bishop of Liverpool, "to be heading for a social crisis, as mutual resentment between the haves and the have-nots builds up. The situation has been neglected, and allowed to deteriorate, for far too long already." The body of the text ran to almost 300 pages of scarcely diluted anger at the attitude of policy-makers towards a highly unsatisfactory status quo. "A high level of unemployment," it declared, "is an evil which has put down deep roots. People who are unemployed feel that they have become invisible, that society is indifferent to them, if not actively hostile." Church-goers, and others in the rural areas, will have readily said "Amen" to that.

Three months after this report was published, the newly elected Government announced measures intended to implement what it called its welfare-to-work programme. Among the unemployed themselves, especially the long-term unemployed, there was a reaction of cynicism with a touch of wait-and-see and among the service providers there was more than a touch of scepticism. For those directly affected the resignation that comes from being out of the work habit, even in pleasant surroundings, will be hard to shake off. To the Government's credit, however, it continued, vocally, to aspire to a fairer society. Its announcement in August 1997 to set up a Social Exclusion Unit was evidence of this.

In late 1996, the jobseeker's allowance was introduced. Under the terms of this allowance, a person who had been registered as unemployed for a year was required to attend what in the countryside were called "rural restart" courses. These courses engendered their own cynicism. One member of a group attending several days of "restart" lectures at a centre in the north of England told me the participants were no nearer "real jobs" at the end. Some of them, he agreed, began to entertain thoughts of going into business on their own account, but others were resigned to taking up gambling in a big way or turning to crime. A year later, this sort of "philosophy" still had its own validity.

A Low Pay Unit report on Suffolk, a county affected both by the peace dividend and the cutbacks in fishing, described the rural labour market in early 1996 as a special case for treatment. It noted that the lack of job opportunities and the relatively small number of employers now operating in the county gave these employers a disproportionate power over the local workforce. While two-thirds of adults were working, and 16 per cent were self-employed, more than 18 per cent were described as economically inactive. The service industries were the biggest employer, taking nearly 27 per cent of the known workforce, though if one includes distribution in all its forms, as well as hotel and catering work in this sector, it is closer to 50 per cent, while agriculture employs just 13 per cent.

But it was the low pay and working conditions of the majority that most struck those compiling the report. Well-paid professionals and managers were co-existing, such is the nature of rural England today, with workers on exceptionally low rates of pay, sometimes living next door to each other in the same village. Seven out of every 10 of those interviewed by the Low Pay Unit were reported to be earning less than £200 a week, compared with just over one in four nationally. The average working week was given as 46 hours, nearly six hours longer than the national average. The self-employed, it was noted, were "no less likely [than the low paid] to be living in a household experiencing poverty".

Some weeks before the Unit published its Suffolk survey, the Transport and General Workers' Union conducted its own canvass of East Anglia as a whole, examining conditions in Cambridgeshire and Norfolk, as well as Suffolk. It found that nearly 200,000 workers in these three counties were earning less than £4 an hour, as were nearly 5 million in the whole of Britain. Nearly three-quarters of all East Anglian women workers were on less than £4 an hour, and rates of less than £2 an hour were "widespread".

In March 1997, the Countryside and Community Research Unit at Cheltenham published its detailed report on developing rural anti-poverty strategies in South-west England. The report, called *Beyond the Village Green*, quoted a local council official based in Cornwall: "The rates of pay are extremely low and the employers down here know that they have the power. My wife works in a village shop. She couldn't bargain for more pay if she wanted. Down here you would lose your job – there's always somebody else who wants it." Another local authority official, who had relocated from another part of southern England, said of Cornwall: "There is high unemployment. You get the impression of certain areas just dying, particularly Cambourne and Redruth and northern parts. I think people have been ground down for so long that they cannot see any way out of it. It has become a way of life for them." In Shropshire, in 1996, the county had 10,631 people registered as unemployed – 6.2 per cent of the workforce. On the other hand, a total of 33,669 households were said to be on income support – with a substantial proportion of the recipients either unemployed or lone parents. Deprivation was such that close to 10,000 children in the county were on free school meals, eating the equivalent of 1,800,000 such meals a year.

The compilers of this report – the County Council – pointed out that the jobless claimant count excluded several categories of people wanting work but not getting it. These included: those disallowed from claiming benefit; those on government employment and training schemes; single parents; people over 60; 16- and 17-year-olds who were neither full-time students nor on schemes; and partners of people registered as unemployed. Up to 10,000 people, it was suggested, could be omitted from official figures as "hidden" unemployed. At the same time, and for a variety of reasons, an unknown number were failing to take up the benefit payments to which they were legally entitled.

In May Molteno's interviews in Wiltshire, it soon emerged that unemployment in the village of Lower Copsley touched the lives of many of its inhabitants. Shirley North, who was running the "ailing" village shop against almost insuperable supermarket competition, told her: "Unemployment affects everybody – 22-year-olds right through to older people. My son is a builder, but eventually only got a job on a pig farm. He toured local towns looking for work, including Salisbury, 28 miles away..."

Diana Farrow, of Wiltshire Community Council, listed the pay rates for jobs available at Devizes Job Centre on 31 January 1996. Her findings were revealing and indicative of the unemployment malaise afflicting many parts of rural England. In a posted list of 17 vacancies, she found that a cattery assistant was being offered £40 gross for a six-day week, an administrative assistant £115 a week, a poultry trimmer £120 a week and a dental nurse £135 a week. At the other end of the scale were a residential home manager, who would be on £335 a week, an engineer on £288 a week, and a plumber on £280 a week.

While the country areas may have less unemployment than the country as a whole, their inhabitants are victims of some important differences. They are faced with a more limited choice of jobs than people in the urban areas; there is less chance of trade union support as trade union membership has fallen; and there is little training, re-training or career guidance. For them, low pay, minimal job security and minimal career possibilities have become the norm.

On top of that, and particularly if they have no car of their own, the unemployed may have to make an expensive trip of several miles to and from the nearest Job Centre or benefit office. The government decision to restrict the postal signing facility for people in rural areas has added a considerable (travelling) expense to their already severely stretched finances.

Where rural people do have work, according to the Child Poverty Action Group, 18 per cent of men and 54 per cent of women in rural areas are on low wages, compared with 8 per cent and 46 per cent nationally. An independent research group at the London School of Economics, in a report published early in 1997, noted that people moving off benefits and re-entering the labour market at this time were typically earning £100 a week – less than half of the national average wage. Re-entry wages, the report said, had fallen by 12 per cent in real terms, largely because wages had been adversely influenced by the proportion of part-time jobs.

It is a sign of the times that tourism is now authoritatively estimated to employ nearly 300,000 people in rural England, while farming, which used to be the mainstay and principal industry of the rural economy, now employs far fewer – and less than half the number that it employed in 1950. Changes in the nature and practice of farming alone are indicators that the countryside, to the resident as well as the casual visitor, is nothing like what it seems to be.

Chapter *five*
Who Are the Poor?

As parents, Mr and Mrs Y are very concerned about the isolation of their two children. Apart from school, they have no contact with other children. Mr Y does his best to juggle with giving lifts to members of the family, but inevitably his children are not able to engage in the types of activities commonly pursued by children of a similar age. So far, the children appear to be mixing well with their peers, but the parents find they are not always able to handle difficult situations when they arise.

A Suffolk family, cited in a
Help the Aged report, 1996

Such are the circumstances of one family in England today. This family is deprived rather than poor, perhaps, but it would not take many tricks of fate to tip such a family over into unmanageably dire straits. A hard winter would make their access track impassable, and redundancy for either husband or wife would lead to financial disaster. Given the environment in which they live, however idyllic it may appear to itinerant beholders, it is hardly surprising that Mr and Mrs Y are not always able to handle difficult household problems when they arise.

Isolation is a major part of their daily lives. For the Y family, the village shop is a car drive away, and the mobile shop is unlikely to call on them, though it may make the end of the track sometimes; the supermarkets, where the prices are more affordable, are beyond reach if the car is not available. Money for social activities can be found, but holidays – like the supermarkets – are generally beyond their reach.

Mr and Mrs Y have a young family and live a mile from the nearest road. Their house is approached by an unmade track, which is extremely badly rutted and suitable only for four-wheel drive vehicles. Even so, the track is frequently flooded after heavy rain, and it is not unusual for the family to be totally cut off in bad weather. They rarely entertain friends and visitors can be put off by the inaccessible location. The family has a car, but only Mr Y is able to drive. His wife has a job which she loves for the social contact that it offers, but apart from work she has little social contact and is unable to take part in many social or leisure activities. As a consequence, she has become very depressed and suffers from this and other health problems. Meanwhile...

Mrs D, a widow in Cumbria in her late 60s, has no car and she lives alone in a village of 300. In her village, as she puts it, there are simply "no facilities". She would love to go out more and meet people, but no buses pass through the village. She has an active mind and would like to go to an occasional concert, or join some sort of interest group or even an evening class. She could take a taxi but this would cost her several pounds, hardly an economic proposition for a pensioner...

Mr H, in Cornwall, was a farm worker until he was made redundant 18 months ago. He is in his late 20s, outgoing and sociable by nature, and he would like to get married. But he has been made redundant before, and even though he has a job as a builder's labourer he feels no security and remains totally uncertain about his prospects in agriculture. The fact that he has been living in tied accommodation, which his last boss wants back as soon as possible, makes his situation even worse. Despite his apparently easy-going attitudes, his optimism is draining away and he is becoming disillusioned.

These people, like the Y family, are all poor in some way, and deprived. They are just a tiny part of the accumulating evidence that poverty, including rural poverty, has increased dramatically in England over the last two decades. On the Government's own figures for households below average income (HBAI), produced by the Department of Social Security, real incomes, after housing costs, of those in the poorest tenth of the population fell by 13 per cent in the 15 years to 1995, a period in which average incomes went up by 40 per cent and the incomes of the top tenth by 65 per cent.

The Child Poverty Action Group, a solid and thoroughgoing research organisation, is not given to hyperbole, even though the area of its expertise lends itself easily to rhetoric. Its pronouncements are carefully weighed and only made when supported by indisputable evidence. In some of its most recent research, it emerges that about a quarter of Britain's population, close to 14 million people, are living in poverty – using the most widely accepted definitions. "Poverty," according to the CPAG in 1996, "is widespread throughout affluent and rural areas."

If poverty is defined, as by many statisticians it is defined, as living below half the average income after housing costs, the numbers doubled between 1979 and 1996. According to figures produced by the Social Security Committee, the numbers had in fact doubled by 1992.

It was in 1979 that Brian McLaughlin embarked on his intensive study, for the Department of the Environment and the Rural Development Commission, of the incidence of poverty and deprivation in five selected areas of rural England. He chose to use a different index, based on the annual gross disposable household income expressed as a percentage of supplementary benefit rates plus housing costs. Using this

In Gloucestershire:
"People experiencing poverty do not talk about it. I have no way of gauging their feelings. Some people (not poor) do now address the problem, others are 'blind' to it."

calculation, McLaughlin said, households with incomes of up to 139 per cent of their supplementary benefit entitlement could be identified as living in or near the margins of poverty.

He was researching before the savage impact was felt of the closure of the country's coal mines, driving thousands of miners on to the dole and taking their families, once their pay-offs were spent, into the totally unknown territory of poverty. McLaughlin found that around one household in every four in the rural areas was living in or near poverty. The worst-off households in his chosen study areas were in Northumberland (27.3 per cent), followed by Yorkshire (25.8 per cent), Essex and Shropshire (both 24.9 per cent) and Suffolk (21.4 per cent).

It is by no means improbable that the same families that McLaughlin described as poor are still poor. But what is beyond doubt, according to the CPAG, is that poverty has increased. In 1994, in its own *Lifestyles* report, one of the RDC's principal findings was that in nine out of the 12 areas studied, 20 per cent or more households were living in or close to poverty. There was, the researchers gently suggested, "a severe problem of rural lifestyle in most areas of the country".

They emphatically rejected the argument that the issue of poverty and deprivation was "an outdated phenomenon" and had become in some way anachronistic in the purportedly prosperous 1980s. The authors acknowledged that, as they conducted their researches, their respondents were on the whole reluctant to admit to poverty or deprivation in their areas. But they also argued that it was a finding of considerable importance that more than 39 per cent of households in the Nottinghamshire study area, 34.4 per cent in Devon and nearly 30 per cent in Essex were in or near poverty.

Away from the social engineer's drawing board, it is important to understand what "ordinary people" themselves see as constituting poverty. One way of doing this is to ask them what they consider are the requirements for a minimum standard of living. The CPAG, drawing on previous surveys that were updated in the early 1990s, said that at least two out of three people thought the following items were "necessities":

- self-contained, damp-free accommodation with an indoor toilet and bath;

- three daily meals for each child and two for adults;
- adequate bedrooms and beds;
- heating and carpeting;
- a refrigerator and a washing machine;
- enough money for special occasions, such as Christmas;
- toys for children.

The CPAG found that one in three of the population – or about 15 million people – lacked three or more of these necessities. These were people who defined themselves as living in poverty.

But the exclusion that accompanies poverty, like the stress that can accompany isolation, is not always immediately apparent and comes in different forms to different people. Farmers and ex-farmers, it is known, are highly susceptible to stress and have an unusually high suicide rate. But lone parents with small children, as well as the elderly and the unemployed, are equally susceptible. Circumstances and opportunities, or the lack of them, can vary from individual to individual, and from social group to group. In the pages that follow, the options and the opportunities are looked at more closely in relation to particular groups whose poor or deprived way of life means that for one reason or another they are excluded.

Farmers and others

The total agricultural labour force, according to the Rural Agricultural and Allied Workers Group, in a presentation at ACRE conference, July 1995, was 622,300 at mid-1993. But this total breaks down to include relatively secure and reasonably well paid individuals at one end of the scale, and seasonal and casual – and therefore insecure – labourers at the other.

More than 400,000 of that total are defined as farmers, partners or directors, together with, in just over a quarter of the cases, their spouses, and more than 45,000 family workers. Only 85,000 of the total are retained full-time labour, a massive drop from the total of 126,000 who were "retained" 10 years before. Of these, the 10,000 or so figure for female workers has remained fairly constant. Another

37,000 of the current total are part-timers – half of them men, half women – while 10 years ago the figure was more than 41,000.

But further qualifications must be applied to any detailed consideration of the rural labour force. Only one farm holding in every five now employs hired labour, and those that are employed tend, once again, to be poorly paid, at the "basic grade". The Council of Europe low pay threshold is the equivalent of £5.88 an hour, while the basic rate in England is £3.83 an hour. Six out of

In Warwickshire:
"Vocational training is invariably urban-based and no worthwhile initiatives have been taken to mobilise or to serve the needs of rural populations. Why can we have distance learning packages for teachers but not for out-of-date typists?"

every 10 of the male workers, and seven out of every 10 women, are on the basic grade.

Where average earnings are above the basic grade, it is as a result of the worker concerned putting in large tranches of overtime – roughly eight hours a week on top of the stipulated 39 hours. At the end of the working day, the average hired farm worker earns only half to two-thirds of the amount earned by the average male country-wide.

The fall in the farm labour force has been dramatic, even since the early 1980s. The *Financial Times* estimated in April 1997 that, in the early 1980s, a 500-acre arable farm would provide a "comfortable" living for a farmer and his family and two or three workers; by 1997, a similar farm would be supporting the farmer with no other workers. An accountant's survey at this time showed that farming was still "prosperous" for the top 25 per cent, who were earning £242 an acre in the mid-1990s, against the bottom 25 per cent, earning only £60 an acre.

Union officials underline that farm work is a dangerous occupation, and that there is increasingly less monitoring of just how dangerous it can be. Statistics show that one farm worker dies every week – a fact which draws little attention. One reason is that Health and Safety Executive staff has been cut back in recent years, with the result that less and less attention is being paid to, for instance, the safety of machinery, and especially baling machinery. The great BSE controversy of the 1990s has led to inquiries into the highly questionable composition of some cattle feeds and some sheep dips and their association with the often fatal Creutzfeldt-Jakob disease in human handlers.

Tiredness on the farm is a perennial problem. In 1994, dairy cowmen were estimated to be working a 53-hour week and tractor drivers slightly over 49 hours, often working completely alone for hours at a stretch. Water and electricity workers, by comparison, put in on average 41 hours a week.

A corollary to any discussion on the plight of farm workers is the plight of many of the farmers. A number have quietly surrendered to the lure of tourism, capitalising on what might be called their rural idyll assets, turning once fertile fields into caravan or camp sites, or barns into tea-rooms. Even uncultivated fields that have been "set aside" to meet EU requirements are now earning their own "income", growing only weeds. Even so, for the majority, farming is by no means a lucrative business: statistics in Shropshire in 1995 showed that an estimated 40 per cent of farmers were eligible to draw income support.

Those who have been able to stick with farming claim in many cases to be working on perilously short shoestrings. For many, it will be years before the long-term affects of the BSE crisis become clear and can be properly quantified. Estimates in the middle of 1996 were that up to 800,000 dairy cows and a third as many older prime cattle over 30 months old were heading for slaughter and incineration. The losses in required grazing and fodder have to be added to the loss of the animals themselves.

It is inevitable that many farmers will go into the red as a result of the crisis, and the National Farmers' Union has been severely critical of the pre-1997 government handling of the crisis, in some cases blaming ministers for individual suicides of farmers. Certainly, some farmers have been made bankrupt by BSE, while others, who may have leeway in other production areas, have moved out of beef altogether. Such radical developments will mean further changes in the use of the land and will damage the countryside. The duration of the European Union ban on the sales of British beef will clearly be crucial, and the stress endured by farmers – already one of the highest suicide risks in the professions – is certain to increase.

Shropshire has been one county among many reporting a notable increase in the number of farmers coming forward for stress counselling. In 1996, the crisis of BSE reached what may yet come to be known as its first peak. Bankruptcies and increasing suicides among farmers were blamed directly in farming circles on the indecisiveness of the Government. Farmers had to adjust to the impact of the disease on an already precarious living, not only in terms of the near-trauma of the experience but also in terms of the heavy financial losses entailed. The fact that young people, in Shropshire and elsewhere, are turning away from farming as a career has added to the stress among the older generation.

"The suicide rate among farmers and farm workers," announced the Samaritans in 1994 (a couple of years *before* the BSE outbreak was public knowledge), "is twice that of the general population, and until recently they were less likely to contact us. Now, we make sure people in rural areas know that we are here." After this pronouncement, and others like it, the National Farmers' Union and the Royal Agricultural Society joined the Samaritans in establishing their own rural stress information network. It was the culmination of some three years of intensive talking by an especially appointed working group, bringing together interested government departments and farming interests. It was billed, such was the flavour of the Government of the day, as a vital link between the industry, government and the voluntary sector – a link needed, in part, to assist individuals living a solitary existence in a whole range of occupations and especially those where the emphasis was increasingly on self-reliance.

The NFU said the new network was meant to co-ordinate what initiatives were in place to deal with stress, especially those helping farmers who felt depressed or suicidal. Part of the rationale behind it was the statistic that, for every known suicide, up to 500 people would feel depressed, and only one in five of these would seek professional help. It was bringing into the open, and promoting sensible discussion of, a problem which a generation previously was not even mentioned.

In Sussex:

"All the evidence in rural areas indicates a lack of training opportunities locally, both in vocational courses and in general adult education. Where training involves travel, and therefore additional expenditure, it often proves prohibitive, especially to the young. 'Lifelong learning' in villages mainly applies to more recreational subjects... There is a lack of non-private nursery provision."

The Whitehall response to victims of an ailing countryside economy has been that more encouragement should somehow be given to the setting up of "small businesses". By 1996, there were thought to be around 2 million such businesses in England, approximately double the number there were 20 years previously. The rural view of that total is one qualified with some doubt.

There is no shortage of consultants willing to act as facilitators to those thinking of going it alone. They offer a great deal of advice and, occasionally, a little start-up funding. But remoteness remains an inescapable fact of life in the countryside. In addition, there are fundamental difficulties in obtaining continuing support, as well as skilled labour. Then there are the relative complications of delivering goods or collecting spare parts over long distances. It adds up to a scenario where it comes as no surprise that rural small business in inexperienced hands may easily fail to get off the ground. At least 10 per cent of those monitored in 1996 were thought to be running at a loss.

The 1990 report of the Archbishops' Commission on Rural Areas, *Faith in the Countryside*, was careful to temper its endorsement of the official view that there should be more "successful" small businesses in rural areas with more than a dash of ecclesiastical scepticism. "However," it noted, "[we] should not hide the shortcomings of small businesses in matters like training, financial control and marketing, where larger companies usually have a better record and from whom a training 'fall-out' occurs. If small scale becomes an exclusive norm for rural areas, it will perpetuate weaknesses in the rural economy which will be dependent on outside intiatives to counteract them."

In mid-1997, some grave reservations about the small business situation were being expressed, both by ACRE and – somewhat unexpectedly – by the Country Landowners Federation. They joined with the Federation of Small Businesses to declare rather ominously that the survival of small rural businesses was under threat unless they were given better advice and resources. A reason for their concern was the decision by the Rural Development Commission to cut down its business advice service, making it no longer available to firms employing fewer than 10 people.

Such businesses, they added, were vital for the future economic development and for the general well-being of rural communities. Many of the small firms were employing only three or four individuals and were supposedly the life-blood of the new, post-Thatcher capitalism. ACRE sought to move in its advisers to such affected firms where the RDC had apparently ceased to tread.

Mothers and families

Among the rural poor, it is always the young mothers who have the rawest deal. Some of them may have a stronger sense of safety and community in the countryside than their opposite numbers in the town, but they also have the additional problems of geographical isolation and, often, more hostile social attitudes to contend with. Sometimes, as recent research has shown, they get discriminated against when they seek access to voluntary schemes intended to help them. But then it seems that in the areas of greatest need, volunteers are least likely to emerge.

"There is no let-up," one woman told Elaine Kempson in 1996. "It's day in, day out. It's the same thing. You get tired of trying to figure out what to cook, or how you will make this money do the job of three or four times the amount, and then you can't do it." Another said: "At night, when you're in bed, you start thinking, how am I going to pay for this or that? By the time I go to bed, I can't sleep – takes me hours sometimes. The doctor gave me some tablets, but I don't need tablets. I need two hundred pounds."

It is usually women who bear the brunt of household responsibilities when it comes to money management. The old-fashioned attitude that "a woman's place is in the home" is more common in the countryside. But women tend to be the ones who control the budget since they do much of the spending; they determine priorities, decide which bills to meet and when. Such "juggling" is a fact of life in the town as much as the countryside, but in the countryside there are some very different, but very apposite, factors to be taken into consideration. The obstacles to a straightforward life are more in evidence in the countryside. There is the non-availability of essential services, for a start. Poor infrastructural services (such as transport, childcare facilities, and so on) may be taken as read. But rarely discussed openly, there is a determination, even where such services may be available, not to be found out and possibly stigmatised. It is essential that this too is taken into account.

Almost all the reasons that are advanced for family breakdown in urban areas can also be applied in the rural setting. Poverty can tear families apart or, fortuitously, may bring them closer together. Material hardship can be just as painfully damaging, and the need to get food, to replace children's, or one's own, clothes or broken equipment mean the same thing in town or country – it can be a matter of doing without or getting into debt. Geographical location is irrelevant when it comes to coping with the expense and the inconvenience of health problems, or cutting down – or cutting out altogether – the costs of the "quality" things in life, such as birthdays or holidays.

The pre-requisites are easily spelled out for the emotional and psychological stress that may have to be endured (often by both partners) in deprived circumstances. If the situation is one that leads either partner into feelings of marginalisation and powerlessness, the stress is that much greater. In many areas, the man as breadwinner has lost his job, and the companionship that that gave, and his standing in the community, as well as his self-respect and identity in all these settings.

The strain on relationships, including marriage, has been enormous. Women's Aid has in recent years been quietly but effectively extending its network of outreach centres in the rural areas, offering support, practical help and advice. The marriage guidance service,

Relate, which handles all other sorts of relationships besides mar-riage, has never been busier. The Samaritans, practiced in dealing with people suffering from depression in all its forms, as well as those who may harbour thoughts of suicide, now has a rural outreach pro-gramme in every county.

Food is a hugely important issue. NCH Action for Children regu-larly revises and updates its findings on the relationship between poverty and nutrition. First published in 1991, it found that one par-ent in five, and one child in 10 who was less than five years old, had gone hungry in the month before the survey because there wasn't enough money for food. One child in four had gone without food in the preceding month because they didn't like what was on offer. But when money is tight, NCH points out, there may be no alternative. On top of this deprivation was the fact that no parent or child was eating the sort of diet recommended by nutritionists for a healthy life.

A fresh survey by the same organisation in 1995 looked into the eating habits of pregnant women on low incomes. This time it found that three out of four "regularly" went without a meal, and more than half had missed one or more meals during the preceding day. One in three of the women said that "typically" she was missing out on one meal every day.

A mother of two living near Oxford told the researchers: "A few weeks ago one Sunday we didn't have any money in the house at all. The cupboards were empty and all we had to eat that day was a boiled egg on toast for the children and a tin of soup between me and my husband. That happens at least once a month and it gets you down. I have gone without myself. If there is only enough food in the house for the children I always make sure they have theirs first, then I make sure my husband has his meal because he works..."

Statistics have shown that women are more likely than men to be living in poverty following divorce or partnership breakdown. Their health – mental as well as physical – can also be more affected by poor quality housing, for the simple reason that they spend more time in the home than men do. If, as single parents, women and their children become homeless, they tend to finish up in poorer accom-modation than men do.

Of course, women in rural areas have different opportunities to change their circumstances, as well as different needs, to those of women in the urban setting. But their opportunities to find and secure work, training or retraining, or simply information, are much more limited. For a start, they can be routinely hampered by a lack of viable transport or sensible child care. Six women out of every 10 in rural areas have no driving licence. An RDC study of women and employment in rural areas (1991) looked at Wiltshire, Cornwall and Derbyshire. It found that while rates of employment were relatively low, the number working on a part-time basis was significantly higher than the national average.

In Wiltshire:
"Access to vocational and adult training is the problem. There is some planning of outreach facilities, but not enough...."

Such women are understandably discouraged by low pay and by insecurity of job tenure. They remain among the lowest paid workers in the country, with average hourly earnings in 1996-97 about £7 – compared with about £8.75 for men. Part-time earnings, for men and women, are approximately level, at just over £5 an hour, but they can be as low as half that amount. Some women's incomes are so low that they do not even qualify for maternity benefit when they fall pregnant.

According to Low Pay Unit surveys, women's pay has gone down markedly since the abolition of Wages Councils in 1993, which at least had a built-in "safety net" for the lowest paid. This drop in pay is despite the fact that, as studies in several rural centres have shown, women are not just earning "pin" money but making a vital contribution to the family budget.

Women also find written contracts, holidays and sick pay harder to get than their male partners. They have fewer savings and smaller pensions than men – though they live longer – and they are less able to buy a home of their own or to rent one privately. A woman with childcare needs can be seen as "problematic" to her possible employer. More than a third of working women have children under 16.

Equal opportunities can be a rarity in the countryside. An innate conservatism on the part of would-be employers has led in some areas to instances of prejudice on several fronts, and even to de facto barriers to setting up small businesses. The Women Returners' Network commented in early 1996 that women's circumstances, *vis-à-vis* employment, in the rural areas was such that "you might at times be forgiven for feeling invisible". It is no longer surprising that women (and indeed men) often finish up in work that nothing like reflects their paper qualifications and abilities.

In February 1996, the Equal Opportunities Commission's Janet Hemsley reported a number of initiatives in different parts of the country to combat the prejudices – though Hemsley used the less emotive word "difficulties".

She found that, in the East Midlands, women in rural areas have initiated groups to raise awareness of the barriers that exist and of the potential that women have to contribute to the local economy. Cornwall has chosen to launch a Businesswoman of the Year competition, while Shropshire has focussed on childcare provision and how it can be improved. In rural areas of the South-east, a series of personal and career development programmes are being developed in the rural areas. As these initiatives begin to bear fruit, it is the Commission's hope that the resulting experience and know-how in combating prejudice will be shared across the regions.

In July 1995, ACRE held a workshop on the theme Supporting Women and Families. Workers from a group called the Durham Community Initiative were given a leading role. They began with a brainstorming session, inviting participants to list the sort of factors which prevented women from taking up training in rural areas. Childcare and transport came top, but their list also included: lack of self-confidence, cultural expectations, lack of provision, lack of motivation, timing, perception, family expectations, lack of finance, lack of jobs, the venue, access, and not being asked what their own requirements were.

This list was candid and revealing enough, but so too was the contribution of a woman from Exmoor who spoke up in a parallel seminar, led by a representative from the National Playbus Association. This woman said that in her remote village the only community facilities were a post office and a pub. This meant that women could become very isolated. One of her circle told her she was only able to leave the farm when her husband was not using their only vehicle.

Another woman in the same village disclosed that she had never been further away than Minehead, 14 miles distant, and had been there only twice. This woman had a son who was three years old, who had never been out of the village and had had no experience of playing with other children. From the other side of the country, in the rural East Midlands, a social worker told of how small children were in some instances growing up barely able to communicate. "They just don't talk to anyone and spend all their time murmuring to chickens," she said.

A year after the ACRE workshops, a small ray of hope for some women came with the publication by the RDC of what it said was a practical guide to good childcare practice, compiled by Jean Scott, of the Kids Club Network. It offered 15 examples of what were described as successful projects in rural areas across the country. The RDC noted pointedly that the different projects illustrated what could be achieved with the involvement of public as well as private and voluntary sectors. In themselves, the projects also demonstrated the important role that childcare could play in sustaining living and working rural communities.

But the sad fact is that only slightly more than 10 per cent of children under the age of eight – that is, less than 700,000 out of nearly 6 million – have registered childcare places. Even these figures only apply to places for children with working mothers. The Daycare Trust says that as many as 100,000 nannies, some of them looking after children from two families, are operating without any formal regulation. Needless to say, it is seeking a system of tighter monitoring. Meanwhile, around 800,000 children under 12 are "latchkey kids", returning to an empty house, on their own, after school. Out-of-school childcare places are available to only one child in every 50.

The new Government announced early in its tenure – in July 1997 – that childcare was a matter of some concern and that measures were needed to improve the provision. At the same time, it spoke of new "opportunities" for single mothers which would give them a chance of returning to the jobs market. But once again, the litmus test in the rural areas would be whether specific rural needs would be taken into consideration. Previous experience, and the fact that true resources were still limited, curbed any excessive excitement about the proposals bearing early fruit.

Deprivation and Disadvantage in Cambridgeshire, a study published by the county council in early 1996, showed that nearly 70 per cent of all women aged between 16 and 59 were either working or look- ing for work. A similar survey in Shropshire, published by the county's anti-poverty working group, found that more than 9,300 children in the county were on free school meals because their par- ents were on income support, and that one working woman in every three was earning less than £70 a week (compared with the national average of one in five).

A number of studies have pointed out the links between poverty and mental health problems and domestic violence. Child abuse occurs possibly as much as it does in urban areas, but is invariably more difficult to measure. In the words of one experienced social worker: "If it's happening two miles down a country lane, nobody knows it's happening. The problem is one of monitoring."

Frustrations over the family budget, as well as working condi- tions, can lead to violence – though the number of cases reported in country areas seem to be fewer than elsewhere. Facts relating to emo- tional turmoil, family breakdown and even suicide can be suppressed, but where difficulties are being experienced, access to family or marriage guidance counselling, for reasons already stated, can be hard to come by. Certainly, however, divorce and separation rates increased dramatically in areas where the mines were closed at the end of the 1980s.

One irony of rural women working for low wages is that their low income may in some ways increase their own and their children's sense of isolation. The demands of work mean that social activities – possibly essential activities where the children are concerned – have to be foregone, sometimes including activities that may be a spin-off from contacts made at work.

At the same time, the absence of women who are working from their more familiar roles in community activities becomes very noticeable. "The women all go out to work," said a Cheshire respondent to a *Lifestyles* questioner. "At one time, the women were the community, all together helping each other." A respondent in West Sussex said: "More women work, which means there is less chance for the women of the village to get together as they used to."

The number of single mothers in the countryside is increasing, as it is elsewhere. The overall picture shows that only one in four of those who have children under five are thought to be working (in 1997), against one in every two married or co-habiting mothers. Nine single mothers out of every 10 in Britain are thought to be existing for lengthy periods on income support, and certainly they are far less likely to have a job than their counterparts in other European countries: in France, more than four out every five of all lone mothers are working, whereas in Britain it is only two out of every five. Many of their problems are similar to those experienced by single mothers in urban areas, but on occasion they can be very different.

In the countryside, problems of transport for a lone parent with small children can be difficult and complex if there is no car and no access to public transport. In a scattered population, sympathetic friends or acquaintances in the countryside are physically further away, and correspondingly more difficult to be in touch with. There may be more of a tendency than there is in the crowded town towards an inexplicable or even illogical ostracism. In some cases, the telephone is a sort of lifeline, but high telephone bills are just as unacceptable in the countryside as they are in the town.

The young ones

> "I don't think being young is very good when there's
> nothing you can do. If you're young and you live in a
> place where there's loads of things to do, that would be
> good, but I if you live here, it's a bit boring. You just
> want to get out sometimes but there's nowhere to go..."

(Fiona, aged 12)

"Nowhere good to go, it's just a little village... It's small, there isn't a lot of people there and it's usually the older people who live there cos there isn't many young people. I'd just like to go somewhere where there's a lot more happening..."

(Jenny, aged 12)

"We're out there and people are having a go at us as if it were our choice to stand out there in the freezing cold and the rain. If we had anywhere else to go we wouldn't be there, would we?"

(Cathy, aged 14)

Boredom and being misunderstood are the key issues for young people in rural areas. For them, more than most, "peace and quiet" can only mean "nothing going on", while "unhurried lifestyle" suggests a sub-existence which is "slow and unexciting". What some may seize upon as "traditional rural values" can be the vehicle for expressing "disapproval" of young people's unacceptable activities and tastes, their points of view and their aspirations.

Fiona, Jenny, and Cathy are from rural Somerset. They were just three of the mainly disenchanted and often despondent young people who were interviewed by Jim Davis and Tess Ridge for the very revealing Church of England Children's Society publication, *Same Scenery – Different Lifestyle*, published in early 1997. The authors concluded that while it is fairly normal for young people to feel a sense of separation from adults as they go through adolescence, for rural young people on a low income, "feelings of powerlessness, lack of privacy and sense of injustice can easily lead to alienation, and these young people may find themselves isolated and marginalised".

The authors concluded that a combination of low income, lack of access to "social space", heightening the young people's visibility in a small population, and conflict with adults can have important repercussions for a young person's sense of belonging. Being scapegoated by adults, and being told, as they were told in one small town, that "they were affecting the tourist trade" by hanging round the streets, only served to enhance the children's sense of being censured and "unwelcome" in their own surroundings. It is hardly surprising to learn that some of them, as young as 13, have started to drink. "If there's nothing to do," said Cathy, "you end up going and getting drunk or something like that."

Young people, particularly if they are poor, feel they have little control over their lives. Official reports into rural problems, including the Government's own 1995 White Paper on Rural England, paid little attention to them. Alienation comes early. If there are activities in their communities that they can engage in, they tend to be planned for them rather than with their co-operation. If they want transport to an event outside the community boundary, they either have to walk or, somehow, secure a lift.

As, after a few years, they embark on the search for a job, or if they want a home of their own, their prospects can be dismal – through no fault of their own. If they are still at school, the choices on several fronts can be almost non-existent, and the school itself may well be a bus ride away. If they want to go on to further education, it can mean a 6am start from home and the almost unnoticed beginning of a process of estrangement from the community in which they have grown up.

After-school activities are, therefore, generally not feasible, and there are correspondingly few opportunities to take up sport, music or the arts with any seriousness. Access to cultural and entertainment events is also limited. And where specialist guidance or support may be needed, that, too, is seriously limited.

Almost certainly, there is no help at hand from a Citizens Advice Bureau, no specialist benefits advice centre, and almost no proper, and essential, counselling in the event of mental health problems. Most tellingly, there are very few specifically youth-oriented services, apart from a handful of outreach workers who may turn up from time to time to try to break the boredom of young people's routines.

It soon becomes apparent that 19-year-olds who have been unemployed since they left school three years earlier, do not make the best mentors for bored adolescents, especially the under-educated. A willingness at least to experiment with alcohol, window cleaning fluid, glue or hard drugs, or to dabble in the world of crime, becomes understandable. The British National Party has been known to trawl the country areas for new recruits.

It is fertile soil in which the feeling of being out of touch with an older generation is easily able to take root. That generation, after all, has quite different preoccupations and can turn apprehensive anyway at the sight of a posse of high-spirited young people together on a dark street corner. In such momentary glimpses there is more than a whiff of the fear of crime itself, something which in recent years has fostered its own political debate and local sense of prejudice.

While reliable published data on rural crime tends to be very scant, figures produced by the police do show that the incidence of crime in rural districts is much less than in urban areas. In 1994, recorded crimes per 1,000 of the population were at a national average of 105. In Suffolk, the figure was 67 and in Norfolk 86, while, for comparison, the figure for Greater Manchester was 143 and for Merseyside 141.

However, according to the Police Foundation in early 1997, the actual rate of crime has been rising in the rural areas in the last few years, and especially in the towns in these areas. The police view is that this rise is attributable in some measure to the greater mobility of the rural criminal and to the persistence of unemployment and unsatisfactorily paid jobs in these areas. The incidence of some specifically rural crimes – also referred to as crimes in a rural setting – has been increasing, with the criminals' preference inclining to the theft of motor cars, farm machinery and livestock.

The National Association for the Care and Resettlement of Offenders (NACRO) examined rural crime in a report published shortly before the 1997 general election. It called, as a matter of urgency, for a government-sponsored review of the disadvantages being experienced by young people in rural areas, for the more widespread use of mobile facilities for "service delivery" where necessary, and said that regeneration grants should be more discriminatingly targeted.

The same report said there had to be a refocusing of rural youth work and that more effort had to be injected into supporting vulnerable parents and helping schools. Finally, it said there had to be more concentrated work on drug and alcohol abuse and, above all, a more serious effort from those responsible to "make it happen".

Researchers have found that the lack of "things to do" – that is, the lack of local leisure facilities, coupled with a lack of transport to reach more attractive activities – means that the numbers of rural young people likely to experiment with drugs and drink are steadily increasing. Partly because local incomes are lower, amphetamines and marijuana, for example, may be cheaper than in the nearest town. But the incidence of heroin abuse has also risen dramatically in recent years in some rural areas. This is partly because some drugs may be easier to obtain in the countryside than in the town; the local vet, for example, may well have a relatively "accessible" supply, in the sense that his premises may not be so secure as those of the average town chemist.

Rural young people who do not drink may have a difficult time socially with their peer group. This applies especially where they may be attending events together at venues where the security and police presence tends to be less than in the town. Those who do drink, as research has shown, tend to start at an early age.

Dave Philips, of the National Youth Agency, has been eloquent on the needs of young people in the rural environment. In a publication called *Nothing Ever Happens Around Here* (1994), he and co-author Alison Skinner pointed out that however closely-knit a rural community might appear to be, the young people's needs tended to be overlooked and their difficulties were not noticed partly because there were apparently so few of them. According to Philips, a young person's sense of isolation was intensified by his or her dependence on adults. This entailed pressures to conform and live according to the "family history", which were in turn intensified by a general lack of opportunity, by a dearth of approved meeting places and "a sense of claustrophobia linked with their actions being too open to public scrutiny".

Philips's view – less widely known than it should be because of the lack of funding for his organisation, but debated by him with great enthusiasm whenever possible – is for people to get closer to each other. He urges that young people and adults should get together more often in common ventures. He would like to see more volunteers or sessionally paid workers given the opportunity and the facilities to run groups for young people in village halls, perhaps working on a "patch" basis. Where distance or isolation is the problem, he advocates a linkage scheme, bringing the isolated closer to one another or to a centre through phone-ins, freephone numbers and eventually computer link-ups.

In a number of larger communities, experiments are being conducted to find ways of galvanising children and young people and getting them more interested in, and possibly influencing, the local authority decision-making process. This has entailed working with groups of young people who are not without ideas but who, in many cases, have become disenchanted with politicians and the policy-making processes. Their prevailing mood has found expression in their feelings of alienation and attitudes of entrenched cynicism. For all the main political parties, the number of young people who declined to vote in the 1997 general election was uncomfortably large, probably running into millions.

Over the years, Save the Children have run a number of projects to "involve" young people in selected local authority areas up and down the country. They have also initiated a series of meetings and publications to help in the formation of youth interest and advocacy groups. Some of these groups are now working in harness with local authority youth "strategies".

In some instances, they have entailed bringing young people forward to engage in face-to-face exchanges with council sub-committees, while others help young people to progress independently, pursuing specific areas of activity interest, such as the environment. In some instances, the idea is that teenagers should meet, possibly in the local council chamber, to gain experience of working in groups or committees, to express themselves and, if possible, participate in decision-making.

Devon, Leicestershire and Hampshire, as county authorities, have led the way in this experiment. Hampshire has set up an Association of Youth Parish Councils, and was able to claim in a matter of months that the results were tangible. There had been a fall in the amount of local vandalism, and a perceptible increase in young people's real interest in participating in some way in community affairs. By early 1997, there were 14 youth councils in Hampshire and the county council said it had received inquiries from councils in many parts of the country interested following its example.

By the end of 1995, Hampshire's association had produced its own pamphlet, vigorously entitled *The Totally Excellent Youth Council Handbook*. The tone and the spirit of this publication contrast hearteningly with the despairing tone adopted by one 16-year-old speaking for his peer group in a rural area of the North of England.

This young man said he was "fed up with living on fresh air" – benefit provision for his age group was stopped in 1988 by Act of Parliament. Another small act of rejection, in other words, had gone its short course, and another step had been taken towards alienation. For his somewhat older companion, however, things were marginally easier. He was able to retort: "At least now I'm 18 I get benefits."

The old ones

One in five of England's rural population is more than 65 years old, compared with one in six in non-rural parts of the country. The rural elderly belong, in many cases, to a group which could be called "the excluded within the excluded". Often, if they have lived in the countryside all their lives, they will be unlikely to have much in the bank or to have private incomes.

In many cases, they will have "made do" during their working lives on low wages – and they are now paying the price. By the time they reach 74, there is a fifty-fifty chance they will be living on their own, and, if they have not moved away from their family, there is a distinct possibility that their family has moved away from them. Age Concern carried out a survey of the elderly in rural areas between 1986 and 1989, in an effort to identify the needs of elderly people and the needs of those caring for them. It was, the organisation said, "a tale of high drama, petty intrigue, solid success, miserable failure, cold empty rooms, freezing buses, beautiful sunlit valleys, high farce, intense seriousness, complete despair and high-flown ambition".

The same study concluded that the growing affluence of many rural areas, particularly in the south of England and in rural commuter belts surrounding large conurbations, had served to hide "the growing disparity" of incomes. A survey by the Anchor Housing Trust, which works mainly with older people, said in April 1997 that while 84 per cent of Britain's older people have central heating, 17 per cent – which is about 1.8 million individuals – said they were cold because they could not afford to use it. Half of those on incomes of less than £75 a week reported being cold.

Age Concern had some good tidings: in one area of the country, it said, a bus had been used as drop-in centre for the preceding two-and-a-half years. In that time, more than 2,000 people had used it as a place where they could get a cup of tea or coffee and have a friendly chat. Its arrival in their village was invariably seen as a regular social event, and in one or two cases led to the spontaneous formation, by some who "dropped in", of their own social clubs.

Most of the rural elderly who are living alone do not have direct access to a car. Those who do have a vehicle of their own which they are still able to drive, and who are living within driving distance of close relatives or close friends – or, indeed, the caring professionals – may be said to be doing all right! But those who are not can be forgiven for feeling distinctly vulnerable when it comes to cuts in the budgets even of statutory services; the cuts that such services have had to endure in recent years have been proportionately much greater than those that have had to be endured by their counterparts in the towns and cities.

A 1996 research paper put together by Help the Aged, in conjunction with the Rural Development Commission, compared government spending assessments for services to old people in 15 of England's most sparsely populated counties with the national average and with 13 inner London boroughs. Once again, it was the uneven, and therefore unfair, methods of centrally-determined resource allocation that came under scrutiny.

No apology is made for returning to the overall Standard

Spending Assessment (SSA) package worked out by central government. Under the terms of this package, rural local authorities were expected (by central government) to spend £417 on social services on each older person in the 1996-97 financial year, compared with £485 per older person in England as a whole and £878 per person in inner London. The result would be less help for people in rural areas, in the form of residential accommodation, day centres, home helps and meals on wheels. There would be just 10.6 hours of home care available in the countryside per person over 65, compared with nearly 24 hours a week for a person of the same age living in inner London.

This package, according to its critics, showed up the total illogicality of central government thinking. Running costs for almost any person-oriented service in the countryside are almost invariably more expensive than in the towns. Users of the service live further apart from one another, making economies of scale almost impossible to achieve. The rural premium that is in fact added by the Government to its allocations for rural areas serves merely to underline the shortcomings of the situation they are meant to be alleviating.

Pensioners are acutely aware of the facts of isolation, marginalisation and powerlessness. Their advancing years, their probable lack of transport, and/or their incapacity will prevent them from playing anything like a full part in the community. But, somewhat poignantly, their limited access to information can mean they do not even know to what extent they are missing out on their legal entitlements.

Little research has been done into social workers' attitudes towards poverty. Their attitudes towards community care and means testing, on the other hand, are clear. A survey published by the British Association of Social Workers in April 1997 said some practitioners in the field actually saw themselves contributing to the poverty of those using their services.

One said that the new Community Care Act was "really a means to tighten and reduce services" and that those who were poor and old were restricted to "little choice" either of services or of residential care. Another social worker said: "Many elderly clients do not get enough home care support because a) they have to pay too much to social services, and b) they cannot buy what social services cannot supply." Even so, surveys of the rural elderly frequently end up with something to say on their special brand of pride. These are individuals who know very well about the stigma that may be attached to poverty or extreme need, such as they may very well be experiencing, but they retain their spirit of "managing". To admit to need or to dependence on an outside agency or even to loneliness is to lose face, to forfeit something very valuable in the way of independence.

One Suffolk response given to the RDC's *Lifestyles* questioners (1994) was: "Some older people would go without rather than ask for what they are entitled to. They are often too proud". A Wiltshire rural community council officer said: "Elderly people particularly do not like to moan. They think they ought to manage and it's very difficult... They work out a very complicated system of how to survive in a rural area... They think that if they cannot get to the doctor and get a prescription, it is just their trouble, and they do not tell anyone." This means that large numbers of older people are evidently either stoical enough or (grudgingly) willing enough to put up with less than satisfactory, even primitive, housing conditions. Close to 400,000 households in rural England – many consisting of single pensioners – were calculated in 1996 to be in housing need. Homes that are still without mains gas or electricity, or, more frequently, without a septic tank, or where the only lavatory is out beyond the back door, are often the homes of the elderly. These homes may have changed little since the present residents started living in them perhaps 40 or 50 years ago.

About 50 per cent more homes in the countryside are in poor condition compared with the percentage in urban areas. The crunch is reached when these homes may have deteriorated so badly as to become uninhabitable for health reasons. At such a point, options are limited: for many of those directly affected, the reality is that property more suitable to their circumstances will either not be available in the places where they would most like to live or it will now be too expensive even to contemplate.

The loneliness and the isolation which can overtake older people in the countryside can be expressed in a variety of ways. The RDC *Lifestyles* survey cited a Wiltshire respondent who felt strongly that more of the business executive "type" and more retired people were moving into the area from outside. "It seems unsatisfactory," this respondent said, "that young people are almost forced away to housing estates where they are cut off somewhat and cut off from family. The whole idea of the family in its supportive role is lost. In turn, the children are not around to support the parents in old age." Another respondent, in Cheshire, put things more succinctly but was equally revealing: "Those coming in are wealthier. Our daughter will not be able to live locally unless new starter homes are built."

Immobility arises usually, but not always, from personal physical incapacity. It may also arise as a result of limited transport opportunities. An Age Concern officer in Lincolnshire reported in 1994: "City-dwellers have no idea of the difficulties faced by residents in isolated areas... Many villages have no public transport links with other villages and towns. Elderly people may have to rely on the goodwill of car owners to get them to main road pick-up points, and then have to wait for a long period in the cold and rain."

For elderly people in the final phase of their lives, the outlook need not be bleak. Peter Tebbit, senior adviser with the National Council for Hospice and Specialist Palliative Care Services, wrote to me in April 1997 of his experiences of several years running a hospice in western England which served a population of around 250,000. Patients from rural areas, he told me, seemed more willing to travel comparatively long distances to the hospice for day care than their city counterparts. Village communities, he had found, were also often more supportive to patients – and their families – who were being cared for in their own homes.

Department of Social Security estimates have indicated that as many as a million pensioners each year may not have been taking up State benefits to which they were legally entitled, so missing out on an opportunity to add, in many cases, as much as 25 per cent to their existing incomes. One reason for missing out is the ignorance of the person concerned about their real entitlements; or their inability to come to the offices of the agency concerned. Some local authorities, and voluntary agencies such as Care and Repair and the Citizens Advice Bureaux, for example, have got round this by introducing mobile information units – often tying in with local meetings on a relevant topic. Other authorities have made a point of assessing needs on a regular basis.

Help the Aged, in a conference on growing old in the countryside, held in mid-1996, did not mince words. Is one courting an idyll or a nightmare? it asked. Its own answer tended towards the latter: many older people, it declared, are "particularly disadvantaged" by living in rural areas. When I wrote in *The Guardian* at this time that if you have the choice of living or not living your last years in the country-side, don't do it, there was not a single letter of protest.

The Government itself, according to case studies drawn up by Help the Aged, has highlighted a discomforting problem. One study centred on a marshy region of Essex, about an hour out of London, known locally as The Dengie, where the population was scattered among isolated villages and farms. Only slightly over half of the households could afford to run a car, and bus services were infrequent in many of the villages. Older people made up 20 per cent of the local population, and the nearest hospital for the majority was 30 miles away.

In this region, such care services that were available were sparse and mainly concentrated in inaccessible towns. It has fallen to local volunteers to retrieve an otherwise desperate situation. The Dengie Project ferries old people about the area, taking them to a newly-formed day centre, taking them on excursions, teaching them "living skills" and how to cope.

Similarly, people who live in the North Yorkshire Dales have devised a *modus operandi* which they have come to call the Dales Partnership Project. This is an area where one person in every four is over 60, but where the nearest neighbour for some people can be miles away, as the population is very dispersed. The situation is made worse by harsh winters, a time of the year when communications can be extraordinarily difficult. However, community-based luncheon clubs in three Dales villages have eased loneliness problems – up to a point – but only perhaps for specific people at a specific time in their lives. In the words of one retired farmer: "In the past, Dales farmers had large families and there was always somebody to talk to. That isn't so any more."

The Whitehall assumption, when it comes to allocating resources, is that only 2.3 per cent of people over 65 in rural areas will need local authority help with residential care. This percentage falls well below the national average and compares with 4 per cent in inner London. The proportion "officially" expected to need home care services is put at 13.5 per cent for rural areas, and 18.6 per cent in inner London; the number of places available in day care centres and clubs is two-and-a-half times higher in inner London than in rural England; and the number of home delivered meals is three times higher in London than in the rural areas.

But once again, the key decisions relating to the allocation of these resources, as Help the Aged and other concerned organisations continuously underline, are made on the wrong criteria. They fly in the face of the fact that older people, whose health needs usually cost more than the needs of younger people, are more heavily concentrated in the rural areas, and the more "rural" the district the greater the proportion of older people tends to be.

The amount of information that could be gleaned on the state of people's health in a given locality – to say nothing of the services and care accoutrements that could be delivered by peripatetic social workers or more district nurses or health visitors attached to doctors' surgeries – has yet to be quantified. It is partly because health and social services agencies seem generally disinclined to work together that hospital after-care schemes are almost non-existent in the rural areas.

Few moves appear to have been made to actively co-ordinate services or information about them. This is in spite of the fact that such schemes are able to save twice their outlay costs by consequentially reducing the number of re-admissions and allowing people to return home at the appropriate time. The best practice in the use of resources – achieved, logically enough, by integrating hospital discharge and hospital alarm schemes – is honoured more in the breach than the observance. It is a context where no serious account seems to be taken of the sparsity factor – in this case, the higher cost of service provision.

It is also fast becoming an area where the voluntary sector contribution has come to be taken for granted or, at best, to be regarded as the cheaper option when it comes to service delivery. There is a clear need for this contribution to be more formally recognised and even totally reassessed. Its activities, where possible, should be costed in advance as a matter of routine and, where feasible, to be given sensible subsidies in the form of revenue funding, on a regular and long-term basis, and grants. "Where do we go," one aged speaker asked at a conference on this subject in London in mid-1996, "if the volunteer ceases to arrive?"

Chapter *six*
Who Cares?

Doctors need to consider their own further development,
and in particular how they will equip themselves for work
as physician, manager, purchaser, researcher, teacher
and educationalist, and epidemiologist. The bad news
is that a GP in a small rural practice may need to be
all of these!

William Cunningham, a GP, and Jean Sargeant,
registered nurse, writing in Occasional Paper,
Rural General Practice in the UK, 1995.

any consideration of health services and community care in the rural areas has to take account of a number of paradoxes. A central paradox, almost an anomaly, lies behind the fact that more and more people are seeking to spend their last years in the countryside, among an already ageing population. Yet while there has been plenty of research into health needs of the urban areas they may be leaving behind them, little substantial research has been done into specific and different health needs in the rural areas. Britain, in this respect, lags behind other developed countries.

Another, related paradox is that at a time when resources for the provision of health care have been subjected to increasing controls, the health authorities seem to have no clearly established policy on the extent to which rurality should be taken into account when precious resources are being allocated. In a carefully argued report on community care in the countryside, published in 1996, ACRE concluded that this has not been given enough attention either in legislation itself, in policy guidance, local care planning or provision.

One result is that, on the rare occasions when serious academic inquiries have taken place, even the most dispassionate inquirers have been driven to the view that resources have often been allocated for political reasons. Clearly, this is a thesis which will have to be revisited as the political changes occasioned by the 1997 general election begin to bite.

Yet another paradox is that while health services are clearly important to a growing number of people in the rural areas, they seem to have thrown up comparatively few pressure groups or lobbyists. This is in spite of the fact that the process is now being completed by which responsibility for community care is passed from central government to the local authorities. As ACRE and other investigators have found, there is a noticeable lack of involvement of the rural population themselves in the relevant decision-making processes relating to how health needs should be met. The way people really live can get in the way of the idyll.

But sophisticated paradoxes and their consequences are of scant comfort to the rural poor or deprived. To them, the chief concern is that the lower down the socio-economic scale they find themselves, the less healthy they will generally be, and their lifestyles are such that they and their immediate dependents will be at risk of ill-health. Any change of government brings minimal comfort in such a situation: deprivation, it could be argued, has been inexorably built into their way of life.

A research programme in Nottinghamshire in the early 1990s started from an initial premise that rural communities should be defined as those which could not get to an out-patient clinic and back in less than half a day. The corollary which surprised them was

In Dorset:
"Social services admits that it only caters for the most needy, and they often have to be bussed very long distances to day centres. There are fewer services here than in most other counties due to a long history of under-investment and a disastrously low funding level."

that, where there was total dependence on public transport, many patients would find it impossible to make such a trip in a one day.

Inadequate research makes it is difficult to say whether country people on the whole are healthier or less healthy than their urban counterparts. What is known, however, is that they are much less likely to consult their GPs. For this and other reasons there can be measurable and serious delays in the rural areas in initiating and following up treatment. Despite this, surveys have shown that although rural doctors' surgeries may be poorly equipped, they are busy. Many are located in private houses or in village halls, and only one in five is in a purpose-built property.

A number of research papers have shown that the costs of providing health care in rural areas is higher than in the town. These costs include: the lack of economies of scale; additional travel costs; additional telecommunications costs; a high level of unproductive time; a slower pace of development work; extra costs in providing outreach and mobile services; and extra costs in training and other support.

In February 1997, in what a senior participant called a unique display of unity and concern, representatives from three Royal Colleges – of General Practitioners, Nursing, and Physicians – met in London to discuss the open secret that poverty in late 20th century Britain can be a significant cause of ill health. Their concern stemmed from the knowledge that people in white collar jobs live longer than those in blue collar work, and the broad acceptance that there can be a five-fold difference in mortality (in, for instance, lung cancer) between those at the upper end of the social scale and those at the lowest.

But even though this conference took place at a moment of general election activity, and health inequality was indeed quite a strong Labour Party theme, the issue was not taken up with any real vigour by the other political parties. If there have been occasional policy directives to reduce poverty, they have not been with the objective of reducing the inequalities of health. The hope expressed at the end of the day's meeting in London was that awareness would be raised among policy-makers of the seriousness of the health situation.

Three years before that conference, a small team of health spe-

cialists, led by Dr Ian Watt, a
health authority professional in
the East Riding of Yorkshire,
said more research was needed
into the health and health care
of the country's rural population. Health and care provision,
it was noted, varied from rural
area to area, and the National
Health Service did not seem to
have any consistent policy

In Lincolnshire:
**"Few hospitals. Many in
towns of 3,000 to 10,000
have closed in the last decade
and some larger ones are
likely to close soon. But there
are masses of residential care
homes – at a price!"**

about whether rurality should influence allocation of resources.
Aneurin Bevan's wish in 1945, that the new NHS should make
"an equally good service available everywhere", was very far from
being fulfilled.

The Watt team underlined that as service provision in the NHS
was becoming more centralised, so the access to appropriate health
care in the countryside was reduced. They spoke of a phenomenon
they called "distance decay", in which distance from a doctor's
surgery was negatively related to consultation rates. In other words,
patients living in rural areas were "much less likely" overall to go to
their GP than their urban counterparts. Mobile provision, they
added, might improve access, but it was also staff-intensive and
tended generally to be a less efficient way of giving treatment.

Reaching the nearest appropriate hospital was also comparatively
difficult in rural areas, especially for the ill who had no transport,
and for individuals with reduced mobility, and/or those who were
either elderly, disabled, parents with young children, or were trying
to manage on a low income. Death rates before arrival at hospital are
higher in rural than in urban areas. A joint report compiled by Scope
(formerly the Spastics Society) and the North Warwickshire Council
for Voluntary Services, published at the end of 1995, touched, not
surprisingly on the strong feelings of isolation felt by parents and
carers in rural areas.

"Parents in country areas," the report said, "find their energy is
drained by the large amount of time needed to attend self-help and
support groups or to take children to medical and therapy appoint-

ments, because of the distances they have to travel and transport difficulties." The services on offer, it went on, had to be more varied, more relevant, and more flexible. "No one should assume," they concluded pointedly, "that professionals always know best." A Department of Health paper published by the Government at the end of 1996 listed some of the good things that were happening in England's rural areas, illustrating its pages with lots of smiling faces. However, the small print conceded that not all was well everywhere. "The closeness of some rural communities," it noted, "offers opportunities for successfully developing services, [but] it can also present problems in terms of the lack of anonymity afforded to individuals."

In some sensitive areas of treatment – relating, for instance, to treatment for mental health problems, HIV, or concerning child protection – the paper suggested assurance should be given of confidentiality, "otherwise people with problems who already feel distanced from their neighbours may resist seeking further assistance". Individuals suffering from particular health problems, and especially concerning mental health, may be reluctant for this reason to join a common interest or therapy group: anonymity simply cannot be guaranteed when it is most needed. But then, it is pointed out by Kay Whittle, of Cumbria Social Services, on the very next page of the same publication, that "traditional patterns of support" based around the family, and especially farming families, have declined.

And there is another factor, which is not actually a sign of deprivation but a sign of deep-seated attitudes towards the unusual. This is the phenomenon of Nimbyism – an infectious disease which finds sufferers unanimously declaring "Not in my back yard" to any allegedly discordant development in their immediate vicinity. It is something which can afflict life-long country-dwellers as much as any newcomer.

In early 1997, there were several reported Nimby outbreaks at once. In the New Forest, the inhabitants of the town of Lyndhurst objected to the use of a converted hotel as a 40-bed unit for people with mental health problems. In Shropshire, the people of Telford protested at an open meeting about a similar project in their area – when it had hardly left the drawing board. In the Basingstoke area, there were similar protests at a proposal to establish a rehabilitation centre for younger psychiatric patients.

The Matthew Trust, a London-based mental health reform group which campaigns for a secure environment for the mentally disordered, published its own findings in early 1997 of a survey of the work of professionals attached to community mental health teams. People with mental health problems, they found, faced appalling difficulties because of low income and problems with the social security system. "Most clients," one team told the Trust, "lead a hand-to-mouth existence, but often face formidable obstacles in getting benefits to which they are enitled. Paid employment, as an alternative to living on benefits, is usually not an option..." What the Department of Health failed to acknowledge in its 1996 paper was that sick people in the countryside are less able than their urban counterparts to choose their own GP and that, where there may be a group practice, the number of doctors may be limited. What, furthermore, if the GP being consulted is a person of "ethical principles" and will not, for example, prescribe contraceptive advice for unmarried women or under-age teenagers?

By the end of 1997, the cardinal role played by health visitors was being used to gain more knowledge of the true circumstances about health in the poor areas. A research project was initiated at the University of East Anglia to ascertain whether regular access to a Citizens Advice Bureau worker had any measurable impact on a family's income, and, as a result on its health.

Chapter *seven*
Who Needs Help, and Who Gives It?

Being in debt is about living on a tightrope where it is difficult to maintain a balance and each step taken risks a fall.

Social Work, Poverty and Debt – BASW Report, 1997

Christmas is a notoriously difficult time for people on low incomes, especially for those with children. One debtline client brings up two young children alone. She manages on Income Support... but she has several debts which stem from the long period that she has had to to survive on a low income... despite her debt and irregular payments to his company, the agent puts pressure on our client to take additional credit each year to fund Christmas. She can't afford to owe any more, she knows that she is paying a high price for goods, but equally she has no access to charity shops or supermarkets, her village shop is expensive, and the temptation is enormous.

Rural Accounts, 1997

by common consent, the army of volunteers who work with the CABs – the National Association of Citizens Advice Bureaux – do an extraordinarily worthwhile job. So worthwhile that it is one of few publicly-supported bodies which briefly saw its funding – like its never-ending workload – actually increase during the 1990s. It was a short-lived moment of pleasure, however. Its body of "district information officers", who peripatetically visit special interest groups, such as the aged and the disabled, was severely cut in 1996.

Nevertheless, the CABs have nearly 30,000 advisers on their books – 90 per cent of whom are volunteers – working in nearly 2,000 main bureaux and ancillary outlets. Between them, they are now handling more than six million queries a year. The demand for the CAB service continues to grow steadily as less and less help becomes directly available from government departments and other agencies.

In 1996, the Department of Social Security decided to close down its highly successful freeline telephone advice service. This had had an extraordinarily active lifespan of a dozen years, and ministers had been prominent at celebrations for its succeeding anniversaries. The service had been a lifeline for people in isolated areas wanting to know the nature of benefits they might be entitled to, and within five years of its launch the service was handling a million calls a year. That lifeline was now cut.

Then, for some families, came the decision from the Lord Chancellor's office in early 1997 to tighten the rules and restrict the availability of free legal aid for suspected criminals. On top of these changes, recent years have also seen a steady decline in the number of "benefit buses" serving more remote communities.

The CABs' own recent figures show that during the 1990s the growth in the number of inquiries relating to debt has been level-pegging with the growth of those relating to social security entitlement. As more and more local authorities have been formulating anti-poverty strategies, CAB advisers have been linking up with local council counterparts to strengthen each other's "lifeline" services. "All the CABs in the county," said the Wiltshire head office in 1994, "are overwhelmed with problems created by the recession, unemployment, low pay and debt."

For those in the countryside who are in debt or encountering other sorts of intolerable difficulties in running their daily lives, reliable advice is a commodity that they can have unexpected difficulties in reaching. The CABs are proud of the fact that their staff are able to provide confidential and impartial guidance on every subject. Records show that most customers (54 per cent) call in person for their advice, and that more than a third (36 per cent) call by telephone.

But such criteria for success apply mainly to urban areas; and they have to be radically overhauled if the rural goldfish bowl syndrome is taken into account. While the CABs themselves may be delighted at the efficacy of their outreach programmes, or that the mobile advice units they are still able to deploy may be serving as many as half-a-dozen villages or more every week, distraught rural customers may have another point of view.

If they step inside such a unit in their home village, they might well find the sort of advice available they so desperately seek. But they have an additional problem: they may be seen, or they think they may be seen, as they step inside. There is a latent fear that the problems they have so far managed to keep to themselves – or, as others might say, have repressed – will become open secrets.

It is a further source of usually undisclosed anxiety, even of shame, to many unhappy would-be customers that they may be known personally to the person who is acting in an advisory capacity. By the same token, they cannot be sure who will come on the line if they call by telephone. If the adviser who finally faces them then talks in terms of having to appear before a tribunal of some sort, the shame can be intensified. Such considerations are also fundamental facts of life in looking at rural deprivation.

For it is this sort of "I-have-my-pride" thinking that sends many rural customers of the CABs to the next village for advice – even though there is the risk that the same problem of being known may arise. A visit to the next village can be problematical if time is precious, or if the children are in any way demanding, or if the customer is a disabled person, or has transport problems. Such factors, including the wish for anonymity, are part of the equation which shows that, at the end of 1996, well over £3 billion of means-tested benefit entitlements a year were thought to be going unclaimed. As it is, well over a quarter of all consultations with the CABs (1.86 million) relate to social security.

When there is an overwhelming problem in a family's life – whether it is poverty, debt, mental or physical ill-health, disability or any other life-restricting affliction – children are among the first to suffer. At such times, says the well-meaning law-maker, children and parents need all the support they can get. Hence the good intentions of the Children Act of 1989, which came into force in 1991. It placed particular emphasis on local authorities providing services to help families with "children in need". It is, the law-makers declared, the most important reform of the law concerning children this century and its aim is to help children in need to get "the best deal possible", so ensuring that "we achieve the very best for this and future generations".

But it is a law with built-in flaws, which are either structural or moral, depending on which way you look at it. A primary weakness, according to research carried out by the Thomas Coram Unit in 1994, is that it does not address the needs of the rural parts of the country. The Act has been written, according to this research, from an urban perspective. It emphasises, for example, the need for a wide variety, and thus a choice, in the day care facilities in a given area. The fact, say June Statham and Claire Cameron, of the Unit, is that in rural areas it may be difficult for parents to have access to any service at all, let alone to choose.

A further weakness is the prevailing notion that children are best brought up, wherever possible, within their families, that there should be no "unwarranted interference" in family life, and that partnership should be promoted between children, parents and local authorities, and that the rights of parents with children being looked after by local authorities will be protected.

That is fine as far it goes. What is not explicitly acknowledged, in this case by the Department of Health, is that a high proportion of parents are lone parents, with all sorts of stresses and needs of their own. The nuclear family of father, mother and one or two children has long since ceased to be the norm. What price, under such circumstances, the single parent's right, under the 1989 Act, to have a say in any decision-making about his or her child? The Act, according to Statham and Cameron, does not set out to address inequality in access to provision.

One of the stipulations of the Act makes it the role of the local authority, where it believes a child to be "in need", to give advice and possibly assistance in providing services to help the family to improve the child's quality of life. Services here include toy libraries, play groups, nurseries and child minders as well as, where problems are more pressing, family aides, family centres and respite care.

And then there is advice. "Often," say the Department of Health guidelines, "some friendly advice can work wonders... There are many volunteer or befriending schemes to help families..." What is more, there is "a simple procedure" for complaints if parents or their children are dissatisfied with the service they are getting.

So, how effective has this de facto revolution been among the most needy? Statham's view is that another structural defect of the Act is that it leaves crucial and highly sensitive definitions to the local authorities. These include the definition of poverty in cases under review – and, therefore, implicitly, the definition of need.

Partly because definitions vary widely, there are lower and more inconsistent levels in the provision of support services in the rural areas. It is critical therefore, according to Statham, that "most local authorities failed to include either low income or rural deprivation as indicators of need". She also finds them guilty of failing to take into account the "particular solutions" that are required in rural areas in the planning of day care and family support services. Models of pro-vision which work well enough in concentrated urban areas are likely to be inappropriate in sparsely populated rural areas.

Somewhat ironically, in view of the supposed revolution that was implicit in the new Act, Statham calls for more work to be done on, and more funding allocated to support, existing "bottom-up" schemes and services, even though they may be small-scale and low budget. This is preferable to the bigger scale fixed-base exercise which may be inaccessible for many needy families. Help should be given with transport – the service should either be taken to those who need it or they should be helped with transport to reach it themselves.

In addition, there should be more flexibility in approach – in, for instance, the creation of more multi-function centres. Education, health, and social services agencies, whether statutory or voluntary, are not seen in Statham's research to be working as closely together as they could. All these, and others, could provide more input, including advice, for such centres.

The Family Welfare Association was founded in 1869 to offer relief for people living in poverty. It is still doing the same work today and, in mid-1997, had more than 5,000 individuals and families on its books. It is in the process of "re-thinking" exactly how services should be provided in rural areas. It is calling for closer collaboration between general practitioners (who have a key role in the countryside, often achieving confidentiality that others fail to attain), health visitors, social workers and community nursing staff and associated workers, with a view to developing a network for early intervention and preventative work. This would notionally reduce the need further along the line for specialist services that are difficult and expensive to provide.

> *In Devon:*
> **"In most rural communities, all of these services would be remote, as would services like the CAB and other welfare and advisory bodies. New techniques are being developed by rural communities to establish their own services, including helplines and local charities."**

Family Service Units is an organisation which seeks generally to advise and help disadvantaged families to "fulfil themselves". It too acknowledges it is not doing enough in the rural areas and would like to to do more. Difficulties are cited in dealing with scattered populations, but some pilot studies are being conducted, in the Midlands, on how service delivery can be improved. One researcher associated with these pilot studies highlighted the special difficulties of the needy in rural areas by saying: "The problems can be the same as they are in urban areas, but if you live in an isolated rural location, there is no escape." Advice on the quantity and the quality of community care that should ostensibly be available, under both the Chronically Sick and Disabled Persons Act of 1970 and the Community Care Act of 20 years later, has been directly and adversely affected by the now celebrated House of Lords judgment in favour of Gloucestershire County Council and the Department of Health in March 1997. This ruling was the culmination of a dispute which arose when the council withdrew care, three years earlier, from 1,500 disabled people who had been assessed as in need under the 1970 Act. They blamed their decision to cut on a £2.5 million over-spend on social services.

But the action was deplored, and its validity challenged in the High Court, by a pensioner called Michael Barry, who was backed by the Royal Association for Disability and Rehabilitation (RADAR). Barry was defeated and the court ruled that the council could use (lack of) resources as a reason for withdrawing services, as long as the customers' needs were re-assessed first.

Barry and his backers then went to the Appeal Court, which ruled in their favour – that inadequate resources were "irrelevant" when it came to providing services. These had to be provided under the 1970 Act and the council had acted "unlawfully" in withdrawing them. The county and the Health Department then went to the House of Lords, which threw out the Appeal Court decision in a ruling which now affects all local authorities in the country.

It means that those people in rural areas who are deprived or dis-advantaged in the meaning of the Act will remain so – assuming reassessment goes against them. It is a situation which can only dete-riorate when council resources are running low. Local authorities will be able to argue to their customers that they are not now obliged to provide home care services for disabled people if they cannot afford to do so.

The consolation for the deprived is that individuals will have the right to register formal complaints if they feel they are getting "less than adequate" services. Representatives of the CABs, of Scope (for-merly the Spastics Society) and other disability advice services have all seen the effect of the Gloucestershire ruling in the nature of the inquiries coming to them. After the ruling, Scope declared that there was now an overwhelming consensus among organisations working with the disabled that new community care legislation is needed. "What you get," said Scope, "depends largely on where you live."

Not that social workers have an easy life in the poorer rural areas. One who is a friend of mine and is of senior rank, with wide experi-ence of working with the deprived and needy in the East Midlands, told me, as I was writing this book, that she got absolutely incensed when people said to her she was so lucky to be working in the countryside. "What they don't realise," she said, "is that as a social worker you spend day after day on your own with only your bleeper for company. There's no question of discussing even the most harrowing problems with colleagues, and that's so important."

Another advice service acutely conscious of the particular needs of the rural areas is Relate, the national marriage guidance service. It claims to have one of its counselling "centres", or an outpost, or simply a room for a few hours a week, available within 20 miles of anyone in the country who needs it.

In the rural areas, it is seeking to develop what may be called a co-ordinated casual approach. This is to meet needs not through a formal appointments-based system but through informality and, where feasible, on a drop-in basis. Where appropriate, these facilities are being developed in village halls or, if such things exist, leisure centres. From mid-1997, and through short-term funding provided by the Lord Chancellor's Department, Relate has also been running a telephone counselling line. Sensible first-step advice is offered for the price of a local call.

Other counselling services are available on an intermittent basis in rural areas, usually advertised discreetly and informally on local public notice boards. This too can be a service which is run on minimal resources and tends to be provided only at certain times at certain places. But, once again, the customer may find himself or herself going without rather than face the possibility, however remote, of being "visible" or in some way exposed.

Recent years have seen the more visible growth of "private" interests in the counselling and advice business. It is a matter of some chagrin among the professionals involved that anyone who chooses can put a counsellor's brass name-plate on his or her front door, and moves are afoot to put a stop to the practice. But in the world of money, and specifically debt, beggars are not yet in a position to be choosers.

Affiliated to the CABs in Norfolk is an organisation called Norfolk Money Advice (NMA), which helps people specifically in local rural areas with their money problems. One of the tools for its job is a specialist telephone debt advice service, Norfolk Debtline.

Another is that it works with the local Rural Community Council, supporting and training debt advisers. Its third, and parallel, aim is that it seeks to raise awareness, locally and nationally, of the wider issues of deprivation and poverty. "Life for an increasing number of people in rural Norfolk," said a joint publication, *Rural Accounts*, which came out in early 1997, "is characterised by low pay, low expectations and poor access to social, leisure, employment, training and service facilities that many of us take for normal."

NMA is refreshingly unbureaucratic in its approach. "Looking back," says the project manager on the opening page of their publication, "I think we were very naive when we launched our telephone debt advice service. When the first client contacted us who did not have a phone, we all remarked on it, and it was the exception that proved the rule.

"But as more and more clients from rural areas contacted us without a phone of their own, we realised this was no exception. In fact, it really brought home to all of us just how desperate people are – that they will queue up outside the village phone box, juggling a mass of papers, scribbling notes and trying not to let other people see what they are doing..."

Being "away from it all" in the countryside, NMA suggests, can for some people be more of a nightmare than a dream. It cites, for instance, a client with mental health problems who lives by himself but has no support, since he is not considered disabled enough to need social services help. Being alone for long periods, he finds himself in a situation where quite mild problems could become huge obstacles. In an urban area, by contrast, he would probably have access to some form of drop-in centre or community facility.

Another client had a long-term disability, had no access to transport, and had a partner who was an alcoholic running up substantial "slates" at the both the village shop and the pub. This reached a point where the pub and the village shop refused to serve either of them – leading him to cope with the personal stigma of debt and alcoholism in his own village.

A third client was running the village shop with his wife. Both of them were often working 50 hours a week, but paying out so much in basic costs (rent, rates, council tax, and so on) that they finished up with less than £30 a week to feed and clothe themselves and to run their (essential) car.

Catalogue companies, according to NMA, have lot to answer for in their activities among the rural poor. Door-to-door collectors more often associated with large council estates in urban areas are also common in the countryside, where a lack of access to alternative sources of credit, such as credit unions, can force people on low incomes to turn to a catalogue as what seems like a life-saver. This type of credit is often expensive in the long run. NMA argues that credit for the poor is always more expensive than for those who are richer – which is the way credit works. People who have got into arrears often need to find a way to keep up their catalogue payments, even if it means cutting out other priority expenses such as rent or food. It is often the only way that clothes for growing children, and larger items such as vacuum cleaners, can be bought – and is therefore essential.

In the late 20th century, more in the rural areas than in the towns, it is arguable that provision for the needy falls far short of what is required and even of what have hitherto been deemed statutory rights. Whether it is because official criteria are wrong, or because resources are short, or even because social attitudes have changed for the worse, what remains of the rich tapestry of English rural life is not always what it seems. The prettiness of the landscape, especially when there are figures in that landscape, can be very deceptive.

Chapter *eight*
Incomers:
Problems They Meet

*Winter in a solitary house in the country, without society, is
tolerable, nay even enjoyable and delightful, given certain
conditions... The spot may have beauty, grandeur, salubrity,
convenience, but if it lacks memories, it may pall...*

Thomas Hardy ,
The Woodlanders (1887)

*We are being taken over by weekenders. They come in
and change everything, and the next thing is they're on
the council.*

Bill Ewins, a Dorset farmer, speaking for "the countryside
lobby", on the eve of a mass march on London.
Quoted in the *Financial Times*, July 5, 1997

at least one in five of England's population already lives in the
countryside, and the proportion is growing steadily. As indicated in
the preceding chapter, although the late 1990s have seen a small
counter-trickle away from the land and some revival of "life" in the
cities – and most notably in London – statisticians still expect that
trends over the next few years will show England's rural population
increasing at twice the rate projected for the population of the coun-

try as a whole. Figures published in late 1996 showed that more than 1.25 million people left Britain's six largest metropolitan areas between 1991 and 1994, a net loss of 90,000 a year.

Not everyone in the "new rural" population is wealthy, but, on present trends and evidence, large numbers of them might be described as "better-off". Many are car-owning and, where they have sailed with the winds of property booms, mortgage-free. They will go on being bolstered heavily by the elderly who have chosen to retire to a favoured rural "beauty spot". To their thinking, there is probably no reason why they should not be allowed to enjoy their chosen portion of what Howard Newby, in a definition of the English landscape, has described as "part of our history and our culture". In 1988, Newby ventured to suggest, in a book entitled *The Countryside In Question*, that identifying with the countryside was an essential part of what it means to be British. In other words, it is self-evidently a very appropriate place in which to "re-locate" for someone who is employed or who is looking for somewhere congenial to spend his or her twilight years.

For the individual involved in the re-locating process, this is a thoroughly acceptable point of view – even though in the mid-1990s there was still an evens chance that for anyone moving into an older property, there would be no mains gas and a one-in-five likelihood of there being no mains sewerage. But from the moment of their arrival, though the new arrivals may not notice, there are wispy clouds on the horizon. They do not always betoken good news.

In the short term, of course, the sunshine is marvellous. Assuming they have adequate financial resources, our new arrivals will zealously set about, where necessary, getting the mains connected and the plumbing brought up to "civilised standards" in their new old home. It will probably be of little immediate consequence to them that they could be displacing people who had lived in this same environment – or even the same dwelling – for a generation or more.

It may take a serious illness or a major accident to teach them that, in the community where they have chosen to settle, the care and health services on which the elderly and the ailing have to depend are declining. They will learn more quickly, especially if their car breaks down, that a number of the erstwhile "everyday" facilities, such as shops, post offices and schools, may also be in the process of disappearing at a disturbing rate.

It is a process, furthermore, only rarely affected by the reactions of the incomers, however influential they may have been in other contexts. Some, after all, have come to the countryside because it is "different", and this may entail going without what many others would consider deserved creature comforts.

Sooner or later, however, these incomers will detect tell-tale signs that the glow of the idyll which consciously or unconsciously beckoned them could be starting to fade. As sure as old age itself, that time will come for even the most undiscerning of the new arrivals. One can imagine them lapsing into sessions of not-quite-nostalgia for the urban environment and the services and the facilities they have left behind, and which they more or less took for granted. In the worst case scenario – not at all improbable – they may begin to suffer from isolation: for instance, when a spouse or partner dies, and when sudden widow-hood is compounded by the fact that the children are too far away to be regular visitors.

In Sussex:
"We regard the hardening attitude of some newcomers against any change in the village – regardless of the merits of a proposal – to be a real threat towards the raising of standards for the less well-off residents. There is strong evidence from numerous public meetings of a selfish, vitriolic attitude from those who believe they have a God-given right against anything that might result in a house, a job, a rural business being provided. Such people are usually articulate, well-off and will always win – unless some way is found to strengthen advocacy for others not so fortunate."

The stridency of the incomers' tone, and the tension which they are able to generate, will vary according to their strength on the ground. In some communities, usually those within commuting distance of the larger towns and cities, the "new" residents can easily outnumber the "old". There are more and more dormitory villages in the aptly-named home counties, in the West Country and in pockets of the south Midlands. But whether the new arrivals speak for themselves in their consideration of service availability, or for their less articulate new neighbours, the point is that they have good reason for complaint. The situation which in all probability now confronts them is quite alarming.

The Council for the Protection of Rural England (CPRE) was founded in 1926. It exists to protect the countryside from "threat", to enhance it wherever possible, and to keep it beautiful, productive and enjoyable for everyone. In its 70th anniversary year, it chose to let loose one of those well-informed blasts for which it has become well known, once again claiming, for those who cared to hear, that the Government of the day was getting its rural development strategy all wrong.

Jobs are being created, the CPRE declared, homes are being built and business premises provided in the countryside, but the flight of people and business from the urban areas is doing little for those in need in the rural areas. "Whether rural development meets rural needs," the CPRE said, "is a gamble, and the countryside is losing."

Planning directives from Whitehall, it went on, were simply not being implemented carefully enough. There were risks that the entrepreneurs, a class which was in favour – for philosophical as well as economic reasons – with the then political policy-makers, were needlessly destroying the very thing, the beauty of rural England, that attracted them in the first place. An area the size of the city of Bristol, according to the CPRE, is being "lost" in this way every year.

It is an important argument, not just for those who wish to protect beauty as the perceive it. It also matters for those who want to make life more, rather than less, viable for people already living in the countryside. It is an oblique way of saying that, in an increasing number of rural areas, the most immediate need is not necessarily for another miniature Silicon Valley to be created in or next to the nearest area of outstanding natural beauty. It is a polite cry that more thought should also be given to the purpose and the declining viability of the shops, schools and even hospitals that have served small communities since anyone can remember.

However, closures and change have characterised the English

rural scene for much of this century. There are any number of villages where the range of shops, services, even of pubs, has gone down dramatically from what the older generation can recall. Market squares which in living memory were hives of activity, employing a gamut of supporting services of suppliers, carters, stall builders, and so on, have become nothing more than "dead" car parks.

Bill Rider, a retired Devon farm worker, was quoted by ACRE in its 1993 annual report. He was pictured in shirt sleeves, stubble on his chin and a self-rolled cigarette between his lips – an archetypal man of the soil. He was able to offer comparisons of his home village of Blackawton in the 1930s with the Blackawton of today. At that time, he said, there had been a blacksmith, a boot repairer, two grocers, two butchers, a post office and a baker. Today, there was only one shop and a post office.

Such is the nature of the countryside as England approaches the year 2000 that Bill Rider's pithy picture could be repeated hundreds of times in all parts of the country. The decline in social and economic activities, in many instances, can be attributed largely to the closing down of such locally important units. Blackawton, and places like it, have been comparatively lucky. In some villages, the rate of shop and other closures has been even faster, even more relentless and, ultimately, destructive. What is more, it has shown few signs of slowing down.

There are approximately 10,000 rural parishes in England today with a population of less than 10,000 each, and a great number much, much smaller than that. In 1991, and again in 1994, the Rural Development Commission sent out questionnaires to nearly all of them, asking about the availability of basic services. The questionnaires were distributed through rural community councils and, sometimes, through the county councils. Meaningful comparisons were possible, because more than 7,800 parishes replied, including more than 80 per cent of those who had replied in the earlier year.

The results are inherently fascinating, but they are a catalogue of decline. They reveal, implicitly if not explicitly, an inescapable harshness about day-to-day realities of English rural life. More importantly, from the social and sociological points of view, they indicate that the less well-off and less mobile, many of whom have spent their whole lives in the countryside, will have increasing difficulties in surviving as services which their parents took for granted continue to decline.

The message of these figures is starkly clear. It is that the infrastructure that held rural communities together, or gave them a semblance of togetherness, is falling apart. The presence of services which were once accessible to large numbers in a given rural location can no longer be guaranteed. If the infrastructure is going, then, inescapably, the superstructure begins to creak and the new "community" (of which more anon), which is more mobile, displaces the old one. The truly rural population becomes very difficult to define and to identify.

More than 40 per cent of all parishes with a population of less than 10,000 no longer have a permanent shop, and a slightly higher percentage have no post office either. Three out of every 10 villages lack the social focus which is provided by the existence of their own pub, almost the same number are without a village hall, and 52 per cent have no school.

This means that in these places there is nowhere that people can come together to discuss a common issue, or to celebrate, or even to talk or play cards or have a cup of tea together. The smaller the parish – which can be interpreted, in most cases, as "the more isolated" – the less likely it is to have essential services. These are parishes where the very features which kept their inhabitants going in the social and economic sense and kept them in touch with each other and with developments of common concern are disappearing before their very eyes.

The village shop has been dealt near mortal body blows with unprecedented frequency. Many that have managed to survive have often done so on shoe-string budgets. A large number have changed character in recent years, acquiring a licence to sell alcohol, for example, or setting aside space to sell videos, "crafts" and souvenirs as well as normal foodstuffs. But in nine parishes out of every 10 where the population is less than 500, the only "shop" is the one on four wheels which calls, weather and vehicle permitting, and if the residents are lucky, at prearranged locations at prearranged times.

In almost every other parish, however, even the mobile shop is not a regular visitor. There are many villages in England today, especially where the tourists and a sprinkling of retirees may converge, whose only retail outlet is the itinerant ice-cream van.

Despite the introduction and occasional enhancement of minimal government grants to village shopkeepers to buy essential equipment, and despite some recent small concessions in the area of rate relief (where the population served is less than 3,000), the number of village shops continues to decline. This has, in large measure, been as a direct result of the growth in number and size of the out-of-town supermarkets and shopping centres. They are able to offer a range of produce which is inevitably much wider and fresher, at prices which can be as much as 15 or 20 per cent cheaper than those asked by the struggling village shopkeeper.

But the development of the supermarket and the hypermarket has also deprived the inhabitants of many small villages of one of their most important social "meeting points", as well as staple foods on their doorstep. For some of the more isolated rural inhabitants, the casual contacts which "happened", and were maintained, at the till of the village shop were their only contacts in the entire day.

Supermarkets or mega-sized shopping centres, which are generally sited close to towns and cities, are by comparison impersonal and overcrowded. They may also be several miles away from home, something which gives rise to important question marks – and headaches – over the availability of transport. In some villages, the only viable bus service has been the courtesy one which carries shoppers to the nearest out-of-town hypermarket. The less mobile elderly, the disabled and those disqualified by age who have not been able to access such buses have been particularly hard hit.

The survival rate of post offices, despite haphazard interventionist flurries by government in favour of rationalisation, has been better than shops; the post office is still – just – more widely available. This can be because smaller post offices, like petrol filling stations, have been able to combine their traditional services with those of a small general shop. In some instances, they have also taken on board a minimal banking or building society facility. Many have been obliged to diversify by circumstance.

By the early 1990s, fewer than one parish in 10 was able to

say that it had its own bank or building society facility. The loss of such facilities continues to cause problems for the less mobile, less well-off consumers.

In Tideswell, a Derbyshire village of about 2,000, there was a surge of outrage during the winter of 1996-97 as the then Halifax Building Society, the biggest in the land, announced and then went ahead with plans made in head office to close down the counter it had maintained for many years in a local solicitor's office. It clearly made no impression on the Halifax management that a partner in the office concerned, and countless customers from the surrounding "catchment area", had warned them that small rural communities in just such situations were already suffering from lack of financial amenities.

In this case, the village's only other bank – whose head office had by then acquired a totally justified reputation for closing down "uneconomic" branch offices elsewhere – was already operating on reduced hours. It made no difference either that local employers (a quarry and a small engineering company) were paying their workers' wages directly into the building society accounts they then held in the village, nor even that the next nearest bank was five miles away and that the bus service was very limited.

A campaign to keep the building society counter operating found ready support in the village, but it failed to satisfy the Halifax board members. They were busy at this time converting themselves into a bank. So the Tideswell counter was closed – one overhead less for the Halifax to countenance. It was a campaign which has been repeated in many small communities, though in the end this one had a half-satisfactory outcome. Within weeks, another, much smaller building society, the Leek, had moved swiftly to open a branch in the very offices that had been vacated by the Halifax. It was a small event, but it was also a reversal of the tide.

As dramas like this one were being acted out in early 1997, an indicative report was published by the New Economics Foundation in London. This warned that, in many instances, the closure of bank and building society branch offices placed at risk the economies of the communities they had been set up to serve. In addition, the National Association of Citizens Advice Bureaux went out of its way to broadcast the fact that, by denying access to current accounts to poorer people and those in debt, "the [banks] were failing to observe both the spirit and the detail in their code of practice".

Rurally situated banks can be just as selective as their urban counterparts in the way they choose to be useful to their customers. In a nutshell, it is on the bank's terms: you take them or leave them. In some areas where they exist or visit, they will only offer loans over £500. For people on low incomes, such a sum may be way above their credit requirements.

But banks are in no way offering a social service. Frustrated customers are left with bleak choices. Either they find themselves forced to borrow more than they need, entailing higher repayments than can be afforded; or they have to move on to seek smaller "borrowings" elsewhere, difficult in the countryside, at expensive rates; or they have to go without. Credit unions have emerged in a few areas, but it is still possible to envisage a stage being reached – such is the steady rate of bank and building society branch closures – where British banks will be obliged to follow the US example, where a local bank branch has to remain *in situ* since it is considered a community's legal right to have one.

In the late 1990s, as car ownership has continued to climb, the Government in London, in its stated endeavours to promote a "living" countryside, blithely maintained that private transport was the "key" to maintaining what it defined as the quality of rural life. That may be the case. But one household in three in rural England has no regular access to a car. Only one parish in four has a daily bus service, but only one in 15 has a viable rail service. And even these figures overstate the case: not all villagers in a given parish have easy access to the nearest bus stop, even in kind weather. Besides this, after six in the evening it is more than likely that there is no public transport at all. This fact itself has social and cultural implications: it can put the damper even on the notion of a night out elsewhere.

Although a number of villages have been able to develop their own dial-a-ride schemes, these have been the exception rather than the rule. A few more have managed to organise their own community minibus schemes, but they too are a rarity. The Rural Transport Development Fund was set up by government in 1986 to assist in the establishment of such non-profit-making schemes, making small amounts of "pump priming" finance available.

Central government has also helped over the years in encouraging the development, occasionally with local authority support, of the postbus service. These services are now operating in more than 225 districts throughout Britain, but especially in the rural areas, carrying people as well as mail, usually in 16-seater minibuses. But the gloomy fact is that fewer than 10 per cent of the services are self-financing, which means that the future of all of them is by no means secure.

Education is complicated and difficult to obtain in rural England. In more than half the parishes below 10,000 and in two villages out of every three with a population of less than 500, there is no school at all. Many of the schools have been forced to close as a result of falling rolls or deteriorating fabric of school buildings or other unavoidably increasing costs since the 1960s and 1970s. In schools that survive, it has become almost routine for a teacher to be axed as an unaffordable overhead.

Only six per cent of the larger parishes have provision for secondary education. While some parents were able in the mid-1990s to claim that, on balance, education services in the countryside have improved, a larger number felt strongly that they have deteriorated. This has been largely as a result of centrally-imposed cuts to local authority funding, which have grown in severity since the recession of the early 1990s. From the Rural Development Commission, the less than palatable view has been assiduously passed to ministers that, as a result of such cuts, small schools will increasingly be unable to deliver the national curriculum. This leads to a vicious downward spiral, since non-delivery, coupled with a continuing shortage of cash, can only lead to further closures.

Too often, shifts towards rationalisation of education provision, like comparable shifts in other public service areas, have yet again failed to take account of the rural sparsity factor, including known educational needs in rural areas. They have also ignored the vitally important social element – of bringing and keeping people together – that is invariably the case when a locally-staffed school finds itself at the heart of a community. Once children have to travel to school outside the bounds of that community, they embark on a small process of alienation from it, and that same togetherness – like their own sense of belonging – begins to evaporate. It rarely returns.

Small childen suffer from shortages or lack of facilities just as much as their older brothers and sisters. Only one parish in 20 had a public nursery school in 1994, and there were hardly any at all where the population was less than 200. Private nurseries existed in about one parish in 10, while a somewhat higher number, especially in the south rather than the north of England, had parent and toddler groups or pre-school playgroups. Otherwise, childcare has tended to grow on an informal basis, unregulated, and heavily dependent on the goodwill and connivance of voluntary groups and, where these may fail, on relatives or neighbours.

The statutory obligations which have fallen on local authority social services departments to identify, define and, where possible, alleviate need – including poverty – under the 1989 Children Act can be difficult to fulfil if resources are stretched to the limit, as they have been in recent years. Nevertheless, the duties are set out: to see to the provision of adequate day care, child-minding and out-of-school care facilities – if necessary in conjunction with education, housing and health departments.

Measurement of "need", in such cases, can be a matter for fraught debate. But, under the terms of the Act, need can include poverty as well as protection from abuse, risk of abuse and disabilities. The alarm signals sound when a child is deemed to be "under-achieving", or failing to maintain the standards expected of other children of his age group.

Roughly in parallel with the decline in education services has been the decline in the traditional services offered by a local library. While four parishes out of every five have the (limited) services of a mobile library for an hour or two a week, less than one in 10 has a permanent library on its own doorstep. In some rural areas (for example, in Norfolk), a lead has been taken in linking up a number of local shops by computer to a central library, but this is a service which may be beyond the logistic capabilities of many rural communities.

It is thus a fair but dispiriting assumption that many thousands of children are growing up in some of the most idyllic villages of rural England unencouraged to use a school or public library, where there is one, though there may be no books on their shelves at home. Their only "cultural" solace may well be that provided by television. Watching TV for a child has the added bonus that it is a way of keeping on close terms with his or her peer group.

The decline in health and care facilities must also be a matter of growing concern, if not to policy-makers, then most certainly to the increasing population of ageing incomers and their neighbours. Surveys have shown that many country-dwellers live where they do partly because they believe the air is fresher and life is less stressful. But no amount of fresh air and stress-free living can halt the ageing process, or alter the fact that a number of these people will have to turn to a doctor or a hospital at some stage in their lives. Parents, single or otherwise, with small children, as well as the disabled are dependent on the availability of medical treatment.

Recent years have seen an increase in the number of general practitioners in rural areas but a decline in the number of surgeries. This is partly because GPs have been hard to recruit, even in some of the most picturesque parts of the country. In 1994, only one parish in six had its own permanently resident practising GP. Often, he or she worked out of a surgery attached to the village hall. While studies have shown that the number of consultations grows according to the number of doctors available, their thinness on the ground must remain a matter of concern for the elderly, the car-less and the disabled.

Only eight per cent of parishes have some day-care provision for the elderly, while only three per cent – less than one parish in every 30 – have proper care facilities for the disabled. The closure of small cottage hospitals has also led to further cuts in provision: only one parish in 50 has its own hospital. Plans for community care arrangements on a formal basis have been worked out in only a small number of authorities.

Pharmacists, who have met important social and psychological needs, as well as the usual health requirements, are also becoming hard to find. Their business has gone to the larger supermarkets, which now increasingly have their own pharmaceutical sections and dispensing counters. Partly for this reason, only one parish in every five now has an active pharmacy. Some of these, in more needy areas, have been able to survive only with injections of government funding. Most rural chemists are of the dispensing variety, rather than independent businesses. Meanwhile, fewer than one parish in every 10 now has its own resident dentist.

Given the incidence of precarious social and financial affairs among so many country-dwellers, it is surprising to find that – in 1991 – only one parish in every 100 had a permanent Citizens Advice Bureau and that only three in every 100 had the services of a visiting one. In studying the responses to the questionnaires I sent out to rural community councils, it quickly became apparent that one of the most common unmet needs is for someone to turn to for personal and/or business advice.

Church newsletters, though circumscribed to some extent by definition, circulate widely, but then 10 per cent of rural parishes now have no "working" place of worship at all; about seven out of every 10 have a church or chapel, but have no resident minister. While the voice of experience from some de facto community elder may be invaluable, really practical local advice, or even the sort of comfort and support that can be provided by a trained counsellor, can be thin on the ground. Scenes, and even acts, of desperation born out of loneliness, of having "no one to turn to", have measurably increased.

Significant moves were launched by the Church in early 1997 to secure tranches of Millennium funding to assist in the refurbishment of old or redundant church buildings in rural areas as community centres. The parish church itself, after all, no longer provides the meeting place it once did. The Church of England's own recent statistics have shown a fall in the number of regular worshippers nationwide to around one million in the mid-1990s, against four times that number in the inter-war years. In the same period, the number of practising Methodists – an important sector of rural society, especially in northern England – has fallen dramatically to 430,000 (precipitating the closure of nearly 1,500 churches) and Baptists to just over 200,000.

In other forms of social refreshment, the provision at rural parish level has also become sparse. Contrary to widely-accepted belief, nearly two villages out of every three now have no village cricket club, and only slightly more have a football team. Such clubs and teams as do exist often have a difficult time in sustaining a viable fixture list. So much for the myth of cricket on the village green: sometimes it happens, but more often it doesn't.

However, one parish in every two does still claim to have "a recreational facility" of some sort, even if it is only a childen's play area. Four out of every 10 still have a village green, but only one in 20 has a swimming pool. Sports fields, the RDC noted, were much more widely available in the villages of the south of England than of the north.

Pubs, as idyll-mongers will be pleased to note, represent an institution which dies hard. Almost seven parishes out of every 10 in the RDC survey still have their own pub – a matter of significance in many rural areas. For the pub, too, is not just a social centre; it is a venue for a whole variety of interest group meetings, choir and drama group rehearsals, and other social functions. But pubs are also significantly changing in character, increasingly taking on extra retail roles, serving bar meals or offering a full-scale restaurant service, or, in some cases, performing post office functions.

Pubs in rural England have become fascinating objects of study in their own right. Some of them have sold out to the "theme" mentality, resorting to a decor perhaps more in keeping with an expectation created by a television soap opera such as Emmerdale than in meeting the needs of more traditional clientele. Many, certainly, have become centres where the rural idyll and the rural reality meet, almost literally, face to face. As Newby (op. cit) has pointed out on more than one occasion, the village publican has started nowadays to lead a rather split existence, serving two very different kinds of customer. One of these is the visitor, the weekender or the unacclimatised newcomer, who may well be occupying that part of the establishment – usually called the saloon – that may have bowed to the inevitable and turned itself into a nicely profitable eating area. The other is the local and regular customer, who ends up tucked into a snug corner of the bar, chatting to an ever smaller handful of familiar faces.

The most widespread non-sports groups in villages – with their own clearly-defined level of importance in many cases for the social health of the community – are, not unexpectedly, the Women's Institutes and the Mothers' Union. For young people, there may be a sprinkling – but no more than a sprinkling – of meeting places for youth clubs, scouts and guides and associated groups. Most parishes have their own recognised notice boards, in or near the community centre or village hall. But such an amenity, according to separate ACRE research, exists for only seven out of every 10 parishes.

Into each late 20th century community, it seems, some crime must fall, and the law-and-order debate has been one which has intensified during the 1990s. However, it is now the "fear of crime", rather than crime itself, that has become a key issue. In this context, it has probably been surprising for new settlers and incomers to the countryside to discover that only one parish in every 50 has a permanently staffed police station.

Ironically, former police houses have been among the desirable – and sometimes not so desirable – residences for sale in country areas. Every twelfth parish, on the other hand, has a police station staffed on a part-time basis. Only one parish in every 50 has an ambulance station.

But it is one thing to determine, as the Rural Development Commission has periodically done with great efficiency, the amount and the availablity of services and facilities – even if it means, in academic terms, resorting to what the RDC itself calls an arithmetic of woe. It is quite another thing to determine, insofar as it is possible, where the real administrative and political power lies in rural areas. This is clearly as much a matter of fundamental importance to those living in poverty or deprivation as it is to everyone else.

What, it may be asked, especially in the context of constantly eroding corners of the social fabric, constitutes a village when all is said and statistically done? When is a community really a community, embracing all diverse interests, as opposed to those of a tightly-knit, discreetly motivated group? And what are the true powers today of that little organism so cherished by English film-makers of the 1950s – the parish council?

Brian McLaughlin, who knows as much as anyone about the mechanics of rural England, has written and spoken a great deal of the crisis of identity in the rural areas. He has pointed out that although the rhetoric of political debate has made much play of the importance of maintaining local democracy and the need for delegation to the most local level, local government reorganisation post-1974 produced administrative areas significantly increased in size. Hitherto distinct and often antagonistic urban and rural councils were forced into single administrative entities.

According to McLaughlin, such an enlargement of local government units, and the subsequent centralisation of administrative functions, have created seedbeds for the cultivation of concern about the future of rural areas. The local government reorganisation which occurred in the shake-up of the early to mid-1990s has done little to damage these particular seedbeds. However, central government proposals – announced at the end of 1996 and backed up by empowering legislation – to give further powers to the parish councils will need more subtle advocacy if the view held by some of the councils, that the proposals were condescending and cosmetic, is to be dispelled.

At bottom, the parish council today is more or less what it has been for more than 20 years. It is more often than not a self-perpetuating body where women, though they are very evident as volunteers in formal and informal agencies, are under-represented. It is also a body whose chair or secretary, usually a man, is responsible for taking down and publishing the minutes of the last meeting. These amount often to sheets of paper covered in almost illegible single-space typing, which are pinned up on strategically-sited, glass-fronted notice boards that are liable to condensation at certain times of the year, so ensuring complete illegibility.

But what else is the parish council, and, of these three entities – the village, the community, the council – which, if any, has measurable power?

The village is probably the easiest to define and is most easily determined by its visible physical boundaries. Its inhabitants, especially those of long standing, will have no difficulty in deciding which is the last house in the village and which belongs to the next village, however close one may be to the other. In the event of *force majeure*, such as a sudden proposal to build a motorway through its heart, or a factory or housing estate on its periphery, a sense of village identity soon emerges.

The precise nature of communities and the roles that individuals are expected to perform in them can be much more difficult to define. Until about a generation ago, they would be dominated by individuals of varying accomplishments who had lived in or near the village for much of their lives. By the 1990s, however, the leading individuals are very different. Their standing in the community may be superficially little changed from that of their predecessors, but they are new creatures, from both the social and the income points of view. The newly-arrived resident, settling into bucolic bliss after a distinguished professional career, may find himself or herself – unwittingly, but not necessarily unwillingly – thrust into a position of strategic importance.

A newly-arrived entrepreneur may wish to appear as benefactor and, in so doing, find himself, whether he wishes it or not, playing a leading part in community life. In many cases, though he may not acknowledge the fact, the remains of feudal attitudes and structures in the area can play into his hands. Like the representatives of the local landed gentry who held sway in a previous era, he may seek to keep a certain distance between himself and the rest of the community, gaining in the process a measure of prestige. His autonomous powers as a local employer who is able to hire and fire enhance these possibilities.

If this entrepreneur happens to be one of the new breed of farmers, his responsibilities may stop at his perimeter fence. But he too has the all-important capacity to hire and fire. He too may therefore find himself gravitating, actively or passively, towards a place in the hierarchical structure of the community.

Parish councils are bodies in a totally different category from communities. This is for the simple reason that they have statutorily recognised responsibilities and fund-raising powers as the third tier of local government. But, if they are any good, they are also representative of and responsible to the community they purport to serve. They have to interact with and reflect the social, economic and cultural interests of that community.

If the overriding concerns relate to community deprivation or disadvantage, or if individuals within the community are suffering, then the council can be expected to take up cudgels accordingly. There were a number of government moves in late 1996 to increase the powers of parish councils in transport provision, crime prevention measures, and so on, and these have been broadly welcomed in the local government lobbies.

These councils are without explicit party political affiliations, and, because they face little or no opposition at election times, they can be self-perpetuating. This has its own advantages as well as disadvantages. But their members are human beings like the rest of us and they respond to need, poverty, or homelessness (for example) within their parish boundaries in different ways. While they are not ostensibly partisan, they do vote like everyone else at general and local elections, and they have party loyalties. This is something that must influence their relations with, and attutudes to, the next highest tier of local government.

In the experience of ACRE, parish councils tend to be dominated by men (whereas in town and city councils, women have important roles) and they tend to be small-C conservative. They frown today, as they have frowned for centuries, on single parents or on gypsies, or on travellers, new or old. As a cardinal rule of thumb, they tend to do what they can to maintain the status quo.

Their innate conservatism reverberates on, and can seriously hamper, good work being done by rural community councils. These bodies (the RCCs), usually operating at county level, are underpinned by modest government funding channeled to them through the Rural Development Commission. Their activities are fostered and encouraged, wherever possible, both by the Commission and by ACRE.

The formally stated role of the RCCs is that they work "to promote the welfare of rural communities by encouraging community self-help, local initiatives and voluntary effort. This process of making changes is to enable people to take charge of their lives through collective action and to decide for themselves what changes are needed in the community." But the fact that RCCs are funded can place them in opposition to parish councils, which are acting, as they always have done, in a largely voluntary capacity and spirit.

Complications inevitably arise when an RCC wish for change in a given situation comes up against a seemingly limitless obduracy, however well intended, in the parish council. The needs of the deprived, if they are not being specifically addressed, can easily be overlooked or forgotten in even the smallest war of attrition.

One result of this dichotomy, exacerbated in some instances by the burden of official financial support, is that the RCC may find itself stifled as a critic when it is being baulked by local conservatism or traditional thinking. This may in turn slow down, or totally halt, the implementation of socially and/or economically desirable projects or may impede the development of equally desirable voluntary activities on a community's behalf. A less than useful knock-on affect can be that the RCC will itself adopt a conservative strategy and, for a variety of expedient reasons, may choose to "play safe" where alternative courses of action seem tricky.

In such a situation, once again, sight may be lost of the more pressing needs of the locally deprived. In this context, as in others previously quoted, it cannot be surprising if there is a noticeable increase in the awareness of this sense of marginalisation and powerlessness that those deprived people may feel.

Chapter *nine*
Incomers:
Problems They Bring

Win a cottage worth One Hundred Thousand Pounds...
Exhausted by the pressures of life in the city? Dreaming
of a country retreat? Ivy Cottage, a charming two-bed-
room Victorian cottage nestling in a tranquil corner of
the Welsh Borders, could be yours... A striking new
feature will be a balcony at the rear where the lucky
winner will be able to sit back and relax in the long
summer evenings.

A Chance to Win... sponsored by Do It All,
The Sunday Telegraph, 9th March 1997

I used to be able to drive my sheep through Wingrave
when I wanted; now I'm just a public nuisance... I have
very few close friends in the village, I have good friends
on neighbouring farms. People in Wingrave are predomi-
nantly yuppies. I used to be on the Community
Association Committee, but I got sick of the people who
moved in... [they] don't really understand farming life; I
can't get on with them.

A Buckinghamshire farmer, quoted in *Reconstituting Rurality*,
by Jonathan Murdoch and Terry Marsden.

Social and cultural polarisation in Britain was well under way, in the countryside as elsewhere, when in late 1987 Margaret Thatcher let it be known, in her own imperious way, that there was no such thing as society. Her own policies of controlled de-regulation of the economy had seen to that. There were some suitably articulated phases of concern for the deprived, but these were directed mostly at people living in the inner cities.

It is heartening that the word "compassion" did manage to get a look-in, from the New Labour side, during the 1997 general election campaign. But whether premature, though worthy, references to compassion will mean an end to the polarisation process must be very questionable. The incoming Government had repeatedly indicated, and with chilling clarity, that its spending programmes would be broadly in line with those of its predecessor. The constraints, in other words, will not go away and the priorities as opposed to methods of dealing with them, will not change overnight.

It has been in the inner cities that the larger and more traditional employers – in heavy engineering and related industries – have created their own wastelands and laid off thousands of workers. The luckier ones of those laid off have been able to buy their own homes from their local council landlords. But many of them are still living in sub-standard, council-owned or housing association-owned accommodation.

A proportion of them have been obliged to remain confined to what have come in the housing trade to be called "sink" estates, each of which has been characterised until now, more often than not, by its share of "hard to let" properties. It remains to be seen whether any of the "sink" effect will be dissipated by the release of funds from council house sales back to the local authorities as the Government formulates its new spending plans.

Inner-city, or post-industrial, poverty is very different from rural poverty. Outer city poverty, however, is something else again. Here, some of those in hardship live so far from the services and facilities of the city centre that they might as well be living in a rural setting. The expense of a trip into town and back again can be enough to give them pause for thought.

But the average town- or city-dweller, even on a sink estate, has the implicit – and often explicit – support of others living in the same urban neighbourhood. He or she knows that there are people in close proximity who may be in the same boat: they too have damp walls, rotting windows, lifts that fail, and alleyways and stairways where fear of crime is endemic and where drug or alcohol abuse may be the norm. There may even be days where they can laugh together in an "Us versus Them" frame of mind at the momentarily ridiculous aspects of their daily lives. Most of the complaints that come into local council offices are concerned with housing.

Isolated country-dwellers, on the other hand, who face the same or equivalent problems have no such solidarity and fewer opportunities for even a bitter spell of shared humour. This is far from saying that other people know nothing of their problems. "Everybody knows, or thinks they know, where everyone's at," is a Derbyshire youth worker's point of view, defining a state of affairs that has negative as well as positive aspects. "In the city," he ventured, "you can be anonymous." The very fact that polarisation has occurred suggests, of course, that Thatcher was right. Loosely speaking, society may still exist – but it lacks coherence. When John Major, succeeding her as Prime Minister, sought to initiate a campaign for the re-introduction of what he called "traditional values" – deriving from mainly Victorian notions of God, the family and civil behaviour – there were plenty of areas of human activity where the 19th century already held sway.

The late 20th century haves and have-nots have learned their stations in life and they have their separate lifestyles, however grudgingly they may have accepted them. They have conducted their lives in diametrically different ways from each other, even though, in the countryside (and less often in the towns), they could well be members of the same community. In today's countryside, they may quite possibly find themselves living next door to each other.

This is not to lose sight of those who could be called the indigenous rural rich. A lot of money has been made by a few people in the less-than-scrupulous buying and selling of disused buildings ("ripe for conversion"), in selling surplus land, or in setting up lucrative rural businesses to satisfy a transient, or newly-settled, population.

Builders and hauliers, as well as the "big" farmers, are able, despite macro-economic ups and downs, to make tidy livings.

In the 10 years that followed the Thatcher pronouncement on the dissolution of society – that is, up to the general election which was to oust her successor from power – expectations were dashed for an increasing number of people. These were the ones who, as multifarious statistics irrefutably proved, found themselves excluded from many activities and possibilities because of the poverty that had sabotaged the lives of them and their families. If there were the *nouveaux riches* and the fat cats at one end of the social scale, there were also the *nouveaux pauvres* and the dispossessed.

In February 1995, the Joseph Rowntree Foundation published an unusually thoroughgoing (even by its own high standards) survey of income and wealth in contemporary Britain. It chose to do so by comparing "dwarfs" (the lowest income groups) with the "giants" on the highest level. Thus, almost at the bottom, we meet a pensioner couple in their early seventies, living in a council house, on a net income of £63 a week – height: one foot four inches. At the top, another couple in their sixties, owning their home, the man on £47,300 a year and his partner on invalidity benefit, giving a total net income of just over £700 pounds a week – height: a preposterous 15 feet eight inches.

It doesn't take a politician or an anthropologist to see that a miasma of cynicism came to pervade the social and political landscape of Britain during the 1990s. It seeped into the thinking of central and local decision-takers, (off-the-record) civil servants, as well as professionals and bureaucrats at every level. It came to many people who thought they had secure jobs and a mortgage which was under control, but who suddenly felt an unfamiliar sense of insecurity at their place of work. But most of all it affected the underclass of the poor, the unemployed, the sick and – more even than most – the rudderless young.

Polarisation, in the rural context, is different today from what it was in earlier times. A century or so ago, it took the form of the lower orders touching their forelocks and hoping for the best. Now, forelock-touching belongs to the past and polarisation has become the gap which has opened up between the indigenous country-dwellers and those who, in steadily increasing numbers, have come to settle in the countryside.

By the mid-1990s, demographers have become convinced that the flow of people away from the urban areas has become a cascade. House sales have been very indicative. In Wiltshire, it has been noted, buyers were paying more for second homes than the average price for a new home "in town". An estate agent in the Derbyshire market town of Bakewell was not alone in his trade when he said at this time that his list of potential clients (mainly from urban areas) seeking three- and four-bedroomed houses in the area had risen by literally hundreds in the last few months. In other country areas, the news is the same.

Interestingly, the people moving into the countryside are mainly aged between 30 and 44, with children. Some came with their jobs, some of them were small-scale self-employed. Some were the retired. Those moving in the opposite direction, from rurality into the urban environment, are mainly young adults, from school-leaving age to about 30. The whole rural population "mix" has fundamentally changed – probably for ever – in a way that it has not changed before.

Until the industrial revolution of two hundred and more years ago, England had been a nation of country people. With that revolution, everything changed: men left the countryside to find work elsewhere. Some took their families with them to other parts of the countryside, almost literally expecting the grass to be greener on the other side. Hence the pockets of Welsh migrants which became established in rural County Durham in the last century. But the more general drift was to find a new sort of work in the towns and the cities.

In the post-industrial era, the flow has been dramatically reversed. In some cases, it may be descendants of country folk who are returning to their roots. But there are also well-to-do folk with "city" ways who are now buying their way into a rural setting. They are investing, in many senses of the word, in a country home with ample parking space and a good – preferably uninterrupted – view.

One effect of this tidal wave has been that some of the most economically deprived parts of the country – such as East Anglia and the South-west – are suddenly witnessing the fastest growths in population. The population of Cambridgeshire, for example, went up by 15 per cent between 1981 and 1991 and is expected to go up by another 15 per cent in the decade to 2001.

Some of the most "rural" parts of the country now have the highest percentage of pensioners – between 20 and 30 per cent of the local population. The consequential strain on a whole spectrum of local services is clear, as is the upward surge in house prices. Those once "affordable homes", with or without roses round the door, for those who would like to have stayed have overnight become the expensive "Dunroamins" and "Hill Views" of those who have just arrived.

A whole new class (there is no other word) of country-dweller has emerged. It consists of people who enjoy and appreciate the countryside all right – but on their own terms. Often they are people satisfied with the sufficiency of their (imported) lifestyles, and they may proceed to insulate themselves from their immediate surroundings, feeling they do not need to communicate. Not all of them, but many of them, have common characteristics, and their arrival, in many cases, has led to predictable consequences.

From the indigenous country-dweller's point of view, the most important of these has been that they not only slow down the flow – sometimes to the point of halting it completely – of affordable homes, but that they also push up rents. Indirectly, they are hindering the further supply of social housing, whether from housing associations or the local council. The eventual outcome is that true villagers can no longer stay in their own village. And one of the consequences is that the social profile of the village or community in question is also changed.

These incomers are people who like to "improve" their properties, adding to the value, through a rural sort of gentrification which might be called countrification. Ultra-lightweight plastic "oak" ceiling beams are now readily obtainable in the bigger do-it-yourself stores. At the same time, the incomers constitute a class which is almost invariably motorised, and therefore able to commute if necessary. They own the means to travel to meet most of their shopping, entertainment and care needs, and can buy, if need be, the education for the children elsewhere.

Members of this *nouveau* class are quite likely to arrive in their new environment with no apparent need for employment, no worries about having to rely on public transport, and no obligation – given their mobility – to help sustain village schools or shops. This means that, as well as helping to reduce the number of (local) people who are dependent on these services, they are reducing the audibility of those, mainly locals, who press the case for them not to close down.

One result, in the commuter villages, is that although the local pub, assuming there is one, may be crowded at weekends, the erst-while sense of community has become unrecognisable, and very possibly a thing of the past. In what is no longer a "living" village, where services have become virtually non-existent, the most visible sign of intense activity is that of large numbers of drivers entering and leaving the station car parks at the beginning and end of the working day.

Of course, in some contexts, the incomers have totally different, and differing, perceptions of the community. If they are in a village, they may well have strong views on the efficacy of the parish coun-cil and its decision-making processes, or on the committees that run local events and festivities on the village calendar. After a decent interval, they may seek, or even "grudgingly" accept, nominations to join such bodies. One result is that there are now parish councils in what has been regarded as predominantly farming country which have no farming members. All of a sudden, villagers who have been living in the same village for years realise that everybody emphati-cally no longer knows everybody else.

Thus, there evolves a new and more complicated polarisation of influences and opinions. This in turn creates its own tensions. A community within a community may take root, or the main com-munity – assuming it still exists – will find that it has been somehow shaken like a kaleidoscope and has taken on a new form. There is the lighter side, as Howard Newby has neatly noted: the village fête becomes an occasion when the newcomers make wine and arrange flowers, while the locals drink beer and grow vegetables.

But there is another side to the picture. What if "the country life" is not, after all, as agreeable even as the one that Newby depicts? What of the incomer who decides that it's all been a big mistake? He or she does not always bring a family support structure with them, and he or she, or any member of their entourage, may sooner or later find that the available "country pursuits" are not to their liking. Inter-pub darts evenings can have their limitations. It begins to dawn that an unexpected loneliness just might become a problem, bringing its own form of suffering and, just possibly, of social isolation as well.

These exceptions apart, there is also the distinct possibility, and in some cases the probability, that outside the parameters of the village fête, the needs of the less well-off, less assertive indigenous members of the community are put to one side. The problems of the unassertive needy may multiply as the needy find themselves even more "excluded" from the very forum which could be taking up cudgels on their behalf. Suddenly, they find they are living in a community which doesn't hang together any more in the familiar and well-worn way that it once did.

In sociological terms, it has almost certainly ceased to be a community in the German sense of the word *Gemeinschaft*. This is where, according to one definition, close human relationships are built on "kinship, locality and neighbourliness, fellowship, a sharing of responsibilities and a furthering of mutual good through familiarity and understanding".

So it becomes almost inevitable that new reasons are added to the long string of others why the outlook has become more bleak for the rural less well-off. They can no longer say to themselves with any certainty that they can become tenants, or even perhaps owners, of homes being built on a new local housing estate. They can no longer rest assured that they will get a job in the factory being built in what may rather grandly be called the industrial estate.

But it is not just that homes in this context may mean almost unmeasurable waiting lists, and that jobs are few and far between. It is that some of the more vocal incomers who have invested in the rural idyll may well be likely to have strong views on the siting of a new housing development and serious reservations about any likelihood that their idyll, or the view, may be tarnished by such developments as a new factory.

So the newspaper competition winner sits on the balcony of his newly-acquired country retreat, basking, as he surely feels entitled to do, in the evening sunlight. Perhaps he or she nourishes thoughts of a precious rurality which has been an English prerogative for centuries. As he does so, he unwittingly underlines, as it were, the words of a recent Archbishop of Canterbury, Robert Runcie, speaking not so long after the Thatcher pronouncement. "The rural inheritance", he said, "is in danger of slipping from our grasp." In other words, there are important component parts of the rural tradition, if it ever existed, which are, like so many village football or cricket teams, being eroded out of existence. The very nature of rurality has itself become difficult to define.

Steps to retrieve the situation are being taken by ACRE and other concerned voluntary bodies, initiatives which will be described in a later chapter. Some of them take the form of endeavours to ensure that the rural poor will be able to escape the danger that they may be elbowed out of sight if central and local policies do not change dramatically. But how important a priority, at the end of the day, is the hard-up single parent or unemployed, unskilled labourer in those corners of Laurie Lee country in the Cotswolds, or in the villages of Wordsworth's Lake District, of Constable country in East Anglia, and a host of other corners of rural England, where the debate is more likely to focus on the sighting of those brown tourist signs which point the way to the Village Shoppe, the craft museum, or the woollen mill or boutique? There is a very real danger that a significant proportion of rural society is losing its say in what happens to them or to the places they live in.

Crowds of seasonal visitors, and car parks bursting at the seams, can of course be highly lucrative phenomena. They yield very useful revenue to individual entrepreneurs in the village. But it is questionable whether they do much to enhance very substantially the local seasonal worker's standard of living, and whether the children of this seasonal worker will want to continue living in a village he or she no longer recognises as the one they grew up in. As I have shown in Chapter 5, the young already have their own reasons for ambivalence anyway.

Some politicians in the pre-1997 government did find themselves able to pay lip service to the poor, including the rural poor – even though the word "poor" itself rarely, if ever, crossed their lips.

John Gummer, who was Major's Environment Secretary, said pertinently that it was up to the planners to breathe "fresh life" into the countryside, but that conservation alone was not enough. "New jobs and wealth are needed in the rural areas just as much as in the towns," he said (in 1993). "Without them, the countryside will wither away physically, economically, socially." These are fine enough words – but by the time they were spoken they were barely audible: the osmotic seepage of the cynicism referred to earlier had long since started.

A footnote can be taken from a not very significant House of Commons debate which occurred in a not very crowded chamber in December 1996. Dismay was expressed in the course of this debate that the "charms" of the countryside were disappearing too fast under concrete. The speaker was David Nicholson, the then member of Parliament for Taunton, who told the House he was determined to highlight a "serious" point.

"The grey wave moving into the South-west may destroy the very facilities which attract retired people to the South-west in the first place," he maintained. "I am not saying that old people who live there should be moved out. I am merely suggesting that at some point in the future we may have to restrict their rights to move in."

To which declaration there is a small clutch of rather nice post-scripts. One is that Mr Nicholson himself had moved from London to the South-west 10 years previously, so presumably he was exempting himself from the strictures he was advocating. Another is that Mr Nicholson lost his seat in the 1997 general election. A third is that, in Cornwall, the lack of affordable housing, directly caused by the moneyed thousands migrating into the county, had also sparked off its own intense and pointed debate. In early 1997, council officials announced that thought was being given to the imposition of a new purchase tax on holiday or retirement homes. The proceeds of this tax, they said, would be used to finance new housing schemes for locals who were less well-off.

Chapter *ten*

Who Gets Housed, and Who Doesn't ?

*The greatest difficulty has been the lack of
awareness both within the community and from
outsiders. The community did not want to accept that
they had a homelessness problem, as it was not visible.
Homelessness was about cardboard boxes. There were
no cardboard boxes on the streets, so there could
not be a problem.*

Carol Treweek, YMCA project director in
North Yorkshire, in *Images* magazine, April 1997

the coming of the railways in the 19th century irrevocably changed the face of rural England. It led to a new accessibility for many villages, but it also gave a decisive boost to perceptions of the rural idyll. There were inevitably increases in population in some countryside districts, but decreases in others. People were also on the move in the opposite direction. In the 20th century, the coming of the motor car has also led to population shifts – again in both directions. In the coming century, the biggest change will come through the advent of new housing. Speculative builders, and the sort of people buying the homes that are erected by them, are starting to change the face of rural England yet again.

In the wake of such developments, the losers are easy to identify. People on low incomes do not buy expensive properties – though they have occasionally been able to sell them. And the plight of the poor has only rarely changed public policies. A 1990 estimate was that 377,100 rural households were specifically in housing need, while house prices in rural districts were anything from 10 per cent to 50 per cent above the national average.

The situation was one which has not changed enough in the ensuing years to reduce the continuing and ever stronger magnetic "pull", or the social and economic needs, which were drawing the disenchanted younger generation and the potentially homeless to the nearest towns and cities. Even the most rudimentary surveys show that an increasing proportion of the homeless on the streets of London and other big cities have come in from the rural areas.

The Council for the Protection of Rural England has always had strong views on the way successive British governments have planned new housing developments. In December 1996, the CPRE announced that Whitehall-orchestrated planning had been responsible for a chronic shortage of affordable homes combined with needless damage to the countryside. The countryside was given insufficient attention in the implementation of planning policies, as became clear during the 1980s, when 70,000 more houses were built in rural areas than was projected at the start of the decade.

In the second half of the same decade, by contrast, just 37,000 affordable homes were provided, as against 140,000 that were required by measures of social housing need. In the South-east, in the same five years, more than six times more affordable homes were required than were built.

By then, of course, many rural villages had already become post-agricultural communities. Motorways, from the conservationists' point of view, have already scarred much of the countryside, just as double-yellow lines have scarred many village streets. Some much-visited villages have been far-sighted enough to build strategically-sited car parks – not necessarily a blot on the local landscape. But others, with or without car parks, are now so congested at holiday periods that they become "no go" areas, closed to traffic. The idyll, it could be said, has created its own ridiculous caricature.

The new houses that are being built in the rural or quasi-rural areas are frequently sited just out of reach of the yellow lines. Thus, by their presence, they are gnawing away the village's own precious green belts. The new owners, however, are unlikely to be too concerned: they are motorised and, if they are not retired, probably commute to work and go outside the village anyway for much of their shopping and entertainment.

The upshot is that villages which may seem dead to the individual passing through, whether on foot or behind the wheel of a car, are no longer a rarity. Those villages where the only other movement is of a car or two using the high street as a through road are no longer unusual. In such places, to see a person moving about on foot can be a mild surprise.

It is a trend which, on present evidence, seems unstoppable. When, towards the end of 1996, central government published its projection that an extra 4.4 million homes would be needed over the next two decades, there were reactions in many quarters of consternation and panic. Some, already ensconced in the countryside, took up and dusted down their NIMBY ("Not In My Back Yard") banners, while others struck up a more coherent – though sometimes rather strident – debate on greenfield versus brownfield building sites.

It is a debate which will run for several years yet, and it has the rural lobbyists constantly on their toes. Not all by any means have been consoled by the fact that some ministers began, very soon after the forecasts were published, to argue that as many as possible of the new dwellings should be constructed in the urban areas. By the spring of 1997, it was apparent that there would indeed be new building in the rural areas, upsetting the lobbyists. A new small town of 5,000 is being planned, for example, in one of the most beautiful corners of Hampshire. Others are planned elsewhere. But there has been no hue and cry to provide affordable homes and, unless there is a radical change in central policies, it seems that few will be built. The rural poor, pretty certainly, will lose out again.

The projected total number of required new homes has been calculated as the approximate equivalent of a 20 per cent growth for every village in the country. The social conflicts that even a fraction of such growth could theoretically generate will no doubt spawn an interesting novel or two, though few will ever equal *Cold Comfort Farm* by Stella Gibbons, who famously got there first in 1933. Such conflicts will only seriously disturb central policy-makers if the grassroots agitation turned into substantial riots – a development which, some say, is not at all beyond the bounds of possibility. To the politically motivated and responsible policy-maker, a home is a home; and more homes are badly needed.

In those rural areas which many locally-born young people are increasingly having to leave if they are to find work and the sort of life they prefer in towns and cities, the cry is invariably for more affordable homes. The rural lobbies say they want sensitive development and that the best laid plans will be those which are wrought in agreement with the (rural) populations most affected. It will be surprising if their wants are satisfied.

By 1979, Howard Newby was already pointing out that planning controls on rural housing had become instruments of social exclusivity. In the years that followed, it increasingly became apparent that planners and planning processes were quite capable of lapses into fallibility, of doing favours for friends and for people of influence, and even of accepting the occasional bribe.

But even as Newby was writing, the type and the selling price of the houses being built in the rural areas, often in "new settlements", were closing the door to people in greatest housing need. The need was clearly exacerbated by the chronic, endemic and growing shortfall in the provision of social housing.

In the countryside, as in the urban areas, the council tenants' "right to buy", introduced in the 1980s, led to the loss of scores of thousands of affordable homes from the public rented sector. Roughly one in three rural council houses were lost in this way, a far higher proportion than in the towns. Since often cash-strapped, locally-based housing associations have not been able to fill the shortfall, a rural housing crisis has been the inevitable result. A target of just 1,500 dwellings for rural housing grants was set by the Housing Corporation in 1996-97. Meanwhile, in the country, as in the towns, a new type of owner-occupier has emerged on the social landscape.

An increasing number of the poor have been forced to draw housing benefit from the State to meet their rent bills. This has been, for many of them, a totally unsatisfactory sticking plaster treatment, but certainly no cure, for their most pressing problems. They have been victims of the poverty trap, where, if they have ceased to be unemployed and taken work, they have very quickly gone above an income "threshold", which leads automatically to a halt in their benefit allowance. If their wages are less than the benefit they had been entitled to, it stands to reason they are worse off working than not working. A job, in other words, may intensify their poverty and do nothing to alleviate it.

As the "right to buy" was being implemented, many rural local authorities began the search for ways to abide by the spirit of the government proposition that new uses should be found for redundant buildings in the countryside. The decision in May 1997, from the Blair administration, that funds accruing from council house sales should remain with the local authority provoked interesting questions as to how the "new" money should be spent: on badly needed repair and maintenance schemes, on rehabilitation of older but serviceable buildings, or on building new affordable homes.

In Warwickshire:
"There is not time or space here to deal with the housing problem, but I can offer some key words and phrases: sale of council houses; absence of rented properties; weekend/holiday cottages; colonisation; gentrification; long-distance commuting; three cottages knocked into one Des Res; 'The Old' Bakery, Smithy, etc..."

At the same time, however, the official plea that new uses should be found for redundant structures led to a variety of responses. Almost inevitably, it led to the emergence of a new breed of barn-stormers. Some of these were incomers, people who bought up visibly neglected or out-of-use barns and, through sometimes skilful manipulation of planning requirements, were able to convert them into something habitable. These were dwellings for the other end of the housing market – homes that were ridiculously expensive and quirkishly fashionable.

But such developments led to their own flurry of written and vocal protests, to the effect that such moves were leading to the destruction of the rural nature of the land where they were situated, as well as the surrounding landscape. But these protests were out-numbered and outshouted (in counties such as Buckinghamshire) by equally vigorous rejoinders from articulate supporters. It was a new sort of civil war for the 1990s.

"Rural settlements [have] come to be increasingly dominated by rather narrow social strata," Murdoch and Marsden reported. "However, once established in a place, these strata are likely to go to great lengths to defend the neighbourhood against further development... An entrenched middle class will fight to exclude others from the village... Moreover, the poor and many traditional rural residents find themselves squeezed out of ever more exclusive villages."

The 1994 *Lifestyles* report found that housing need was important in all the 12 areas that were scrutinised. Very high proportions of the people surveyed – as high as 90 per cent in North Yorkshire, and more than 60 per cent in all other areas except one – thought local people were experiencing difficulties in getting the sort of accommodation they wanted. Young people in particular were experiencing the greatest difficulties, and the limited availability of rented homes was raised in all areas.

New Age travellers, an increasingly visible phenomenon in the late 20th century, have found it harder and harder – like the gypsies who, over centuries, preceded them in a similar choice of nomadic life – to find a site where they would not be disturbed and where they could pitch their sometimes ramshackle vehicles and live in peace. The Criminal Justice and Public Order Act of 1994 removed the onus from local authorities to provide them with special sites.

Before that Act, only 40 per cent of councils were providing such sites anyway. One of these councils had sites to accommodate just 15 out of 200 known eligible traveller families. In January 1996, a survey by the Department of the Environment showed that there were nearly 10,000 "gypsy caravans" on authorised council and private sites in England, as well as precisely 2,887 on unauthorised "encampments".

The net result of the new legislation, according to Derek Scott, an academic researcher at Bristol University, writing in 1995 with Barbara Perez, an experienced local educationist, is that travellers and gypsies have been subjected to harassment and removal.

Travellers and gypsies have themselves told me, in sheltered hideaways in the relatively affluent south-east of England, that it remains "normal" for them to be subjected to mindless racial abuse.

Local legislators, often claiming to have local public opinion behind them, have frequently been more than ready to dismiss such people and their mobile homes as a blight on the landscape. In late 1996, Chesterfield Borough Council in Derbyshire was driven into surrounding a local industrial estate with deterrent earth mounds. But these were merely ploughed through by the individuals who wanted to live there: the industrial estate, declared the local newspaper, was turning into a no-go area.

An early 1997 survey of procedures being followed elsewhere had local officials relating that the councillors whom they served were apt to dismiss travellers as "being outside the law and... wholly undeserving poor". One official said: "It's not like the disabled, where everyone agrees that they are worthy of our support."

Interestingly, a study in Scotland during 1996 investigated three sites "which appeared to be well run" and found "the problems experienced by site neighbours were far less than they had anticipated". A small number of farms and businesses had reported continuing problems attributable to the close proximity of the sites, but even these could have been reduced through careful discussion at an earlier stage.

Housing has been a sector of perennial concern to rural Women's Institutes. As far back as 1918, when Lloyd George issued his call for "homes fit for heroes", the WI was campaigning that there should be an adequate supply of "convenient and sanitary houses". That, too, was a time when the speculative builders were encroaching on rural territory in search of quick money. Sixty years later, the women were passing resolutions that were critical of legislation adversely affecting the availability of rented accommodation.

In February 1995, the Rowntree Foundation reinforced this view with its pronouncement that the reduction by successive Treasury ministers of the subsidies to local authorities and housing associations had gone "too far" and that the rents being charged by these bodies to tenants should be moderated. Income inequality, it noted in the same social policy report, had grown rapidly throughout the

1980s, and in 1990 had reached a higher level than any recorded since the Second World War.

At the beginning of the 1990s, the private rented sector was bigger in the countryside than in the town: one household in every seven, against one in 11 in the urban areas. Another Rowntree report, published in late 1996, found that households with two adults and childen were more prevalent in the rural private rented sector, while lone parents were less prevalent than in the towns.

A smaller proportion in rural areas were living in furnished accommodation, and four times as many were in unfurnished accommodation, compared with urban areas. Many more households in urban areas shared bath or shower facilities than in the countryside, but many more rural households were living in what the statisticians call "non-permanent accommodation", such as caravans or converted railway carriages.

Citizens Advice Bureau workers in Wiltshire reported in 1996 that they had come across cases of a young girl sleeping in a car, and of young people (unspecified) sleeping in a derelict warehouse or in the woods outside a town. The CAB, itself working out of a converted potato store, was mainly preoccupied at the time with unemployment in the area and low pay. However, a drop-in centre for the homeless – opened with financial backing from local authorities, Crisis and various housing associations, and offering meals, washing facilities, clean clothes, advice and counselling – found ready takers.

In the holiday area of west Dorset, the local CAB found that affordable rented accommodation was "virtually non-existent". In the vicinity, meanwhile, holiday-makers could rent a 17th-century, Grade II listed cottage – or, rather, three knocked into one – with direct access to Hardy's Egdon Heath, for £800 a week. A converted farmhouse in Bridport would cost £1,100 a week.

The disappearance of tied accommodation for farm workers has been highlighted in May Molteno's conversations in the Wiltshire village of Lower Copsley in 1993. "Farm cottages used to be all for farm labourers," Louise Marshall told her. "Now farms are being bought by other people." Pat, in her late 20s and with two small children when Molteno talked to her, said she and her husband couldn't afford to live in the village any more and were trying to move away. They had lived with her parents-in-law for three years and had been on the council waiting list, but got nowhere. Now she was living in a house that was visibly crumbling in places and riddled with damp.

Everyone in Copsley, Molteno reported, bemoaned the lack of people working in the village. But it was hard to stay, almost solely for the reason that there had been a decline in available houses. "In Copsley," she concluded, "there's no option of moving to a better house in the village. If you can't buy, you can only move out."

This is a conclusion that could be reached in many villages in rural England. In the Derbyshire village of Tideswell, a small poll was conducted in the community in connection with Agenda 21. Local people were asked what were the best things and what were the worst things about the village: at the top of the "worst" list, ahead of the financial viability of local shops or the proliferation of yellow lines, was the knowledge that "my children will not be able to afford to live here".

A survey on housing in Gloucestershire, entitled *Who Can Afford It?* and published in early 1997, spoke of the attractiveness and the relative wealth of the county and said that the fact that rents and income were generally "above average" meant that housing opportunities for those on the lowest incomes were very constrained. In Cheltenham and Cotswold in particular, the Cambridge University compilers said, high property prices and lack of supply at the lower end of the market effectively excluded lower income households from the owner-occupied sector and from much of the private rented sector.

The survey detailed those thought likely to face the biggest problems with affordability. First, there were those at the very bottom of the pile, usually single, younger people who cannot easily get access to social housing and who face severe problems with finding and being accepted for private sector accommodation, unless they can prove they have a high enough and steady income.

Then, it added, "for the quarter or so of young single people who are unemployed, the possibilities of securing accommodation are particularly limited. Homelessness among this group is a very real concern." The Gloucestershire problem is by no means unique.

In the housing sector, a parallel sort of blight been has evident in some of the country's bigger rural communities. In early 1995, the RDC said a survey of 131 English market towns had shown that many of their centres in, or near to, a state of decline.

There has been some nibbling at the problem by the National Agricultural Centre Rural Trust (NACRT), which was established in 1975 and works, as a charity, along with some other voluntary agencies, to make more affordable housing available in rural areas. It has set up a series of local housing associations, which, by 1993, had completed 1,500 homes in some 200 villages. In Devon, the community council has created its own land bank to acquire plots of up to one acre on which can be built six or more houses. These ventures go ahead only on condition that the housing remains available for local people in perpetuity. Northumberland has followed Devon's example.

An RDC report in 1992 said the incidence of rural homelessness had tripled in the preceding four years. Most homeless applicants with local authorities in rural areas have been aged under 30 or over 60. A large proportion, as other surveys have shown, are poor and reluctant to articulate their powerlessness and low self-esteem. But homelessness in rural areas is not a tragedy just for the individuals directly concerned; it can also undo some of the residual cohesion of the community where it occurs, changing the economic and social fabric of a village or township.

Problems associated with ill-health among the homeless, including mental health, have markedly increased. This is an issue complicated by the fact that, although the obviously homeless individuals and families may have often only poor access to primary health care services, GPs may be unwilling to take them onto their lists. As a result, children suffer in essentials – in, for example, the poor uptake rate for immunisation.

Helen Sudlow is a health visitor who has been working in Herefordshire and has made a special study of local homelessness and young parents, including single parents, living with their children in approved bed and breakfast accommodation. During researches conducted in 1992 and 1993, she learned much about how the underclass lives.

One Herefordshire mother, living with small children in bed and breakfast accommodation, told her: "We have to keep all the food in the bedroom or else it is pinched, and it goes off and smells in there." Another said: "There's nowhere to prepare food, and feeling hungry is the worst part". A third said: "The kitchen is too dirty to make up baby's feeds. I do it in the sink in the bedroom." A number of Sudlow's clients spoke to her of their frequent bouts of loneliness and depression, of having no one to talk to and nothing to do all day except wander round the local shops. They described their bed and breakfast accommodation as more like a prison than a sanctuary or safe haven, and said they were routinely not allowed to have visitors. Loss of weight and boredom, according to some mothers, contributed to their deteriorating health.

Sudlow pinpointed shortcomings in both central and local government dealings with the physical and mental health problems of the rural homeless. Significantly, a government *Health of the Nation* paper, issued in 1991, made no reference to homelessness in smaller towns and rural areas, even though the Rural Development Commission had publicly highlighted it as a matter for increasing concern. Sudlow also noted that "poor communication between health services and local authorities frequently compounds the problems of the homeless and their families".

In late 1994, the Housing Associations Charitable Trust published its own report highlighting the lack of housing provision for people with special needs in many rural areas. Drawing on the English House Condition Survey of 1986, it stated that a total 559,000 houses in rural areas, more than half of them owner-occupied, were in "poor condition". In addition, the Trust warned that "there is a substantial amount of hidden homelessness in rural areas, particularly among single people".

Shelter's representatives in Lincolnshire have formulated a definition of rural homelessness. "It includes families who need their own home but who are forced to share with relatives. This usually means overcrowding and, in the worst cases, mum, dad and children staying in the living room, sleeping on the settee and the floor. It also includes people living in dilapidated and often damp caravans – of which there are hundreds in Lincolnshire alone.

"It also includes families living in bedsits or in run down and overcrowded bed and breakfast accommodation; it includes many single people forced to stay on friends' floors and, when the friends' goodwill has been exhausted, sleeping rough; and it includes many older people occupying their own properties which they cannot afford to repair, which means they finish up, with deteriorating health, living in one damp downstairs room."

The situation in Lincolnshire in 1993 was that nearly 20,000 households were on council waiting lists but this was only part of the story. Research has shown that more than half the rural households in need fail to register, which suggests, according to Shelter, as many as 30,000 households in Lincolnshire alone were in desperate need of a decent home. Even a conservative extrapolation of these figures for all the counties in England would come up with totals that would chasten many policy-makers, and not only in the Department of Health.

It was also Shelter, as ever at the front in the housing needs debate, that drew important threads together at a national conference it organised on rural homelessness in late 1995. In the published account a year later, Jo Lavis, of the RDC, provided some telling statistics. She said research had shown a need for 80,000 units in rural areas to house people on low incomes; only 13,000 had been provided. Furthermore, in the period 1989-92, homelessness had risen more sharply in rural than in urban areas, and, against the national trend, had gone on rising in the two years to 1994.

Instances and conditions of overcrowding are not as horrific now as they once were. But if too many people are living close together in an unnaturally crowded environment, there is inevitably friction and stress; relationships breakdown and chronic health problems emerge. Young and single people in rural areas have, in recent years, been experiencing the greatest difficulties in securing suitable accommodation. Many local authorities were not registering people under the age of 21 and were not providing hostel or other emergency accommodation. Approximately one in every eight of the households accepted as homeless are in rural areas.

In its own survey of the growing requirements for new social rented housing in the rural areas, ACRE has estimated a need for between 23,000 and 37,000 homes a year for those its housing team were now calling "rural refugees", to be provided either by the local authorities or by housing associations. In March 1997, it drew attention to the cuts in Housing Corporation funding for affordable housing: an overall cut of nearly 40 per cent, announced late in 1996, leading to anticipated cuts in the rural social housing programme – from 1,500 homes in 1997 to just over 1,000 in the following year.

In July 1997, the RDC produced a lengthy assessment of young people and housing needs in the rural areas. Under the heading Policy Implications, its message to the new Government was that even after taking account of the clear evidence that not all young people will choose to remain in rural areas, there was still not enough housing to go round to meet their specific needs. Increasing the supply of rental accommodation, said the team of researchers – from York University – remained a priority.

Tightrope walkers among the fund-holders at the Housing Corporation are, of course, aware of the nature of the problem. "The countryside," said the Corporation's Steve Ongeri, at a housing conference in September 1996, "should not become an executive ghetto. Richer people want to live in small villages, but that choice should also apply to poorer people." A number of independently-forged schemes were operating by the end of 1996, but still the scenario of need – as Chris Holmes, of Shelter, pointed out – was growing with disconcerting speed. It is all a very long way from the vision encapsulated shortly after the Second World War by Aneurin Bevan as housing minister, when he spoke of "the lovely features of English villages where the doctor, the grocer, the butcher and the labourer all lived in the same street".

Chapter *eleven*
Communities Matter

Waverley, in balmy stockbroker-land, is far from being the most grim council area in Britain. But the cooks, gardeners, chauffeurs and farmworkers who have lost tied accommodation at the end of their working lives now depend on the council for homes as they cannot possibly afford to buy the humblest cottage in an area where £250,000 is barely enough to get an estate agent to return your call... In affluent rural areas, the poverty of the minority is made worse by the wealth clotted round them.

Comment, by Sandy Mitchell,
Country Life magazine, 27 March 1997

more needs to be said on the nature of communities and, given the nature of social change in the countryside, some key questions have to be addressed. When does a community come into being? What are its main purposes in local life and whose interests should it be serving? And, most difficult of all, when does a community cease to be a community? If there is such a thing as a community "motor", what sort of blips and breakdowns can be expected, and what can be done to achieve more effective performance?

Anyone who has had cause to linger more than a few days in a village or some other rural setting, however thinly populated, will soon acknowledge the social, cultural and, where discernible, economic complexity of their environment. They will also notice that "communities", even a few miles apart, can be very different from one another. Using the word community in the broadly acceptable sense of a group of people, large or small, who live in a place with commonly-agreed geographical and social boundaries, it is possible – and probably fair – to describe some places as friendly and some as unfriendly. People of different social or ethnic backgrounds may mix, or they may not. People of different incomes may, or may not, feel uncomfortable in each other's company. Given the growing and unprecedented diversity of "rural" villages and communities, detecting who is who in a rural setting can be a tricky business. It goes without saying that perceptions of "what is going on" can vary according to the individual's standing in the community, just as much as according to his or her personal point of view.

Conversely, if an intrinsically important position, in the community context, changes hands – the vicar, say, or the clerk to the council, the pub landlord or the post office manager – then there may be consequential shifts in the loyalties and allegiances felt among members of that community. Community politics with a small P can engender just as much campaigning, intrigue and passion, and can lead to results that are just as fascinating as party politics with a big P.

This means that anyone who may want to "do something" about solving a community's problems has to tread carefully; the community, or the individuals most concerned to change or influence the status quo in that community, may need or want help, but they are people too. And if their problem has been something they may have felt to be stigmatising, or something they haven't usually talked about, or kept hidden even from their closest neighbours, then these facts too are of paramount importance.

The constraints of poverty, even feelings of marginalisation or powerlessness, do not mean there is no latent wish to change the prevailing state of affairs, either at individual level or in the wider context. People's incomes, like many of their immediate needs, can be measured. So can the high prices in the village shop, the lack of everyday services, the shortage of jobs, of affordable homes, and so on. Gangs of kids, large or small, who hang around the bus stop or the war memorial, tell their own story as eloquently as any mothers' group or dole queue.

In Buckinghamshire:
"Parish meetings reveal very significant levels of opposition to any proposals for affordable housing, to the extent that some villages have and will become exclusive ghettos for the affluent. Some parish councillors do not appear to take their responsibilities seriously. One said: 'I don't think people round here would accept housing association schemes near to them.' A good example of exclusion is the young man from L— who took the initiative on an excellent paid restoration project for the village (a Rural Action award winner), but cannot afford to live there himself."

The other side of the coin is the evidence that there are people, including people in need, who have access to transport. This means they have access, too, to the help they need and are able to go outside the community to make the contacts they require, very possibly in the sort of privacy they most want. But their actions may have side-effects: estranging them as people from fellow community members and running down the community's own available services, as fewer individuals make use of them.

Incomers, on the other hand, as I have noted elsewhere, are a different category and have different expectations and needs. Some continue to live their lives separately from their "fellow" community members. But others, where a strange blend of community inertia and community mores permits, may become movers and shakers – as well as good mixers – who will be able to get things done on the community's behalf and with the community's consent. (Such people have been immortalised in the BBC radio serial, *The Archers*, in the person of one Linda Snell...) The coherence, and the vitality, of a community can depend on such people.

But a scenario along these lines cannot be created overnight. Rural communities in many parts of England have been through turbulent times of change in recent years, but – and this may be part of their supposed charm – they have not lost what might be called their conservative characteristics. Not all the changes, by any means, have been welcome, but some have. One result is that prescriptions for mutual aid or self-help may work well in one setting, but not in another half-a-dozen miles down the road. The level or receptivity can vary; some communities will turn their backs, while others will go all out to take advantage.

Self-help and self-reliance mean different things to different groups of people. Projects to set up a new network or interest group, whether it is a move to oust the local council or to set up an informal mums and toddlers' group, may seem fine on the back of an envelope, but that is no guarantee they will take off. Public spiritedness comes easily to some; for others, anonymity is a way of life they may need, or even treasure. The wish to be unrecognised and throughly private can be the very reason that some people choose to "become" rural.

Research suggests that mutual aid works best when those participating in a goods or services exchange scheme are independent by nature and not seeking too much for themselves. By the same token, local voluntary activities can sometimes "take off" when there is a dearth of specialist or professional help available and people simply have to help themselves. (The other side of this coin is that a lack of specialist help or services can also have a negative impact, and lead to lower expectations and less self-reliance.)

Volunteers, ranging from those who represent big organisations such as Oxfam, Help the Aged, or Mencap, to those who run the local drop-in centre or outreach youth group, are increasingly playing key roles for individuals and communities in need. But these volunteers too, especially when they are not resident members of the community where they are operating, need tact, circumspection and sensitivity. They have to "fit in", but also have to retain a measure of independence as service providers.

Having identified needs, volunteers – or paid workers – must take care that no one who is inarticulate or in any way marginalised is excluded from the services they may be seeking to provide. Nothing for the poor or deprived is alleviated if they feel in any way patronised, or if their over-riding impression is still one of exclusion.

This said, there are of course communities where the tradition of self-help is strong – with or without the voluntary input – and can be as near as possible, in a conservative society, to being all-embracing. Whether out of habit, or out of the "good idea" idly floated by an incomer, the list of activity groups, which can be measured by the number of uses or expected uses made of actual or projected village halls, can be rich and diverse. Luncheon clubs may (almost by definition) be exclusive, but playgroups need not be; music appreciation or local history clubs may be self-defining, but baby-sitting rotas and sessions facilitating the exchange of children's clothes are less so.

Support groups, sometimes under a less explicit label, can have built-in problem areas. If, for instance, they are intended to cater for individuals with physical or mental health difficulties, there may be the danger that those whose difficulties are deemed "too severe" may be excluded. This is a problem which would not arise so readily in a larger urban area, where there might be an alternative group to turn to. But the rural goldfish bowl, where one or two key persons may have the power to make important decisions affecting an individual's happiness and/or social standing, offers no such alternative.

In 1988, a rural research group of the Tavistock Institute of Human Relations looked at some mixed rural areas in England, asking themselves specifically: *Self-Help in Rural Areas – Is It Different?* The group's answer was that, at the very least, self-help had to be built on different, and unexpected, premises. It spoke questioningly, for instance, of what it called "the myth of the "caring community" in these terms: "Voluntary and statutory services often put forward a picture of rural life as being one in which villagers look after their own. While this may, in many villages, be the case, this view had also been found to have been used in situations where there was evidence of quite severe need amongst some sections of the community."

International aid workers who have worked in the poorer countries of the world and in the poorer parts of Britain have no doubts about the parallels that now exist between the economic systems used in the countries of the industrialised, or post-industrialised, world and the others who are less well-off. The so-called "free economy", they say, has in both contexts created its own wealth-owning class, its own great layer of small business people, workers and operators, as well as, at the bottom, another layer of the poor.

Oxfam, which entered the international aid scene at the end of the Second World War, embarked with a number of sister organisations on a specifically UK programme in 1994. Philosophically, it started from the premise that, while the scale of poverty varied around the world, it was no longer possible to make simplistic comparisons between developed and developing countries. Desperate poverty and vast wealth (Oxfam's adjectives) were found to be living side by side in Britain, as well as in Brazil. It hoped, therefore, to share its international experience and understanding in its work with organisations and communities struggling to tackle poverty and its root causes in Britain.

"In the UK," it said in a policy statement two years after the programme started, "despite the growing prosperity of many people, a sizeable minority find themselves marginalised and vulnerable, powerless to effect change in their lives – a situation similar to that experienced by many of the poorer people Oxfam works with in other countries." On this basis, five priority areas of action have been chosen: to strengthen social organisation and capacity-building with groups and communities who feel marginalised; to develop ways of responding to the specific needs of women, as well as to those they share with men; to influence public and political attitudes to poverty and inequality; to strengthen the analysis of poverty by using the international perspective; and to address the links between race, poverty and exclusion.

In working with other organisations, Oxfam has made it plain that it wants to give priority to those whose work is based on "new" ideas. Since poverty is more than the absence of material goods or basic services, but also a state of powerlessness in which people are unable to control many aspects of their lives, the aim is to tackle poverty from a holistic, rather than a single-issue, perspective.

One way of doing this is through what is called participatory appraisal, a technique which has been used since the early 1970s and, most notably, with rural communities in countries such as Indonesia and Zimbabwe, but which embodies principles that are considered equally valid for rural areas in late 20th century Britain. Teresa Cresswell, who has a co-ordinating role with the North Derbyshire Health Authority, has used it in areas where she has found that social isolation, limited access to health and social care, lack of pre-school provision and lack of "anywhere to meet" have been the prevailing problems.

The technique has grown out of a concern to involve community members in research as well as decision-making. Cresswell's equipment, in addition to a knowledge of the basic "facts" relating to an area, consists of a notebook and pencil. She starts, she says, by questioning relevant professionals about areas of concern. Thus, health workers of all sorts are asked to identify their "worries"; schools about attendance and educational opportunities generally; social workers about child care and child abuse; police, community workers and the clergy about "social difficulties"; and local councillors are asked for their opinions – and their support.

She then "looks for herself", comparing what she sees with what she has been told on the doorsteps and by those who provide the services, and eventually arrives at an identification of the main needs. Members of the community are then allowed to decide how they want to tackle the problem, so ensuring their "ownership" as well as their participation. Out of this grows the all-important process of empowerment. Community members who were consulted have said they were "very happy" with the results.

But there have been problems with the outcome. The professionals felt the sample gave a biased perception of services, that the sample was too small anyway, and that it had yielded nothing "new". In addition, management was hurt by the negative feedback, and its commitment to change methods was vitiated. Some community members complained about the lack of resources put their way to effect change, while others were apparently so accustomed to powerlessness that they refused money they were offered because they felt their spending plans might not be approved by more powerful people above them. However, on the positive side, community "action groups" have evolved, single mothers have got together to work on common problems, and new friendships and support networks have emerged.

Not surprisingly, Cresswell, who trained as a nurse and worked as a health visitor, concedes that in many situations the concept of "community" can be difficult for people to understand, and that anyway people are not necessarily altruistic. "When people struggle with adversity," she wrote in 1996, "they have little left to give. The old saying 'When poverty comes through the door, love flies out of the window' sums this up well. People have problems in meeting their own needs, and often feel as though they are getting nothing back for themselves. This is why the concept of community does not function as well as we might want."

Tilly Sellers, at Hull University, has worked with the East Yorkshire Participatory Rural Appraisal Network. She too emphasises the "completely voluntary" element in local input, insisting that they should be regarded as "main subjects" and not as "objects of research, planning, implementation and evaluation".

She adds: "This means that, amongst other things, there should be:

- a recognition of local people's capacity to analyse and plan;
- respect for local perceptions and choices;
- a focus on the application of the approach for future improvements;
- a use of visual material, rather than written material only;
- an emphasis on the importance of feed-back and verification; and
- a recognition that information belongs to the participants."

Communities, urban or rural, and interest groups to which they give birth, have a problem if they have nowhere to meet. They need premises that are as affordable as they are adaptable, that are universally accessible, even for the disabled, and that are warm in winter and comfortable to use. They also need a modicum of understanding of regulations and statutory requirements, for the fabric of the buildings themselves – which are often a legacy of the Victorian or Edwardian era – has to be sound as well.

But there are signs that the village hall, of which there are 8,500 in Britain, is coming back into its own. In early 1996, glasses of elderflower wine were raised by jumble sale organisers, advice-givers of all sorts, parish councils, Women's Institutes, and a host of others to mark the news that the Millennium Commission in London had seen fit to give £10 million towards the cost of renovation and rebuilding of village halls falling into decrepitude and disrepair.

ACRE, with support from the Rural Development Commission, made the original submission, applying initially for three times the sum that was finally advanced. There was even some thought given to applying, jointly with Scottish, Welsh and Northern Irish counterparts, for five times as much, for an all-British village hall programme.

The aim of the programme now under way is to renovate or rebuild, sometimes from scratch, as many as 400 halls in time for the Millennium. A survey conducted a few years earlier had found that more than half the country's halls were more than 50 years old, and that two out of every three were "inadequate" to meet the various demands being placed upon them.

These demands are many and varied: ACRE research has found that close to 400 different activities are conducted on a regular basis in village halls. Suggestions that the advent of television would put a stop to many of them were apparently greatly exaggerated.

Further research has shown that as much as £35 million worth of free voluntary labour was being made available each year to run those halls that were already in use. The fund-raising, in the words of an Oxfordshire community council member at that time, never stops. The spectrum of need for access to the hall – for meetings and special interest groups, as well as social events of all sorts – becomes ever wider.

At a subtle, social level, a "good" village hall or community centre clearly has to be available to all who have good reason to use it. The less organised and the less coherent members of a community, like the less well-off and the deprived, may be marginalised, but they too have good reasons to meet, whether because of their very specific needs or to air common grievances and decide on appropriate action. They also have a right to a say in how the building is managed.

Chapter *twelve*
European Dimensions

Beware of romantic neo-ruralism

Delegate to EU conference on rural affairs,
Cork, November 1996

Like poverty itself, Europe has been a sensitive subject for British Government policy-makers. At times it has been handled discreetly, even covertly and sensibly, but sometimes with an attitude of dismissive distaste. Supporters of the cause of the European Union, like those who demand a fairer deal for the undeserving poor, have been labelled, at worst, as extremists (as was the Labour Party leadership during the 1997 election campaign) and, at best, as misguided.

There has also been a measure of reciprocity in the slanging stakes from the European side. In October 1996, as British ministers were refuting notions of poverty in their time, so Padraig Flynn, then EU Commissioner for Social Affairs, was touching raw nerves in London by questioning the nature of the British administration's "support" for the vulnerable poor and the elderly. Britain, he maintained, was engaged in a "heartless and misdirected" attempt to erode European support for such groups.

The change of government in London in May 1997 led almost overnight to changes in attitudes to Europe. The central question here is whether it will lead also to changes in attitude to the vulnerable poor. As Commissioner Flynn was to acknowledge within a few weeks of that election, economic growth and progress do not seem to be "a sufficient condition for social cohesion".

Statistics from the European Commission, published in May 1997, showed that Britain had some of the poorest regional areas in the entire Continent, and it named South Yorkshire, Merseyside, Cornwall and Devon. Britain, on these figures, also had one of the lowest per capita incomes (at £10,270 a head) and by far the highest proportion of under-16s living in poor households.

Recent estimates are that about 57 million individuals of an EU total population of around 370 million – more than one in seven – are living in poverty, earning less than half the average net income. The total of the member states' registered unemployed is at least 20 million (up from 8 million in 1980). A quarter of Europe's population, meanwhile, lives in its rural areas, which in turn account for more than four-fifths of the EU landmass.

Europe's agricultural and rural departments are currently in a state of some turmoil. For years, they have been dominated by arguments about the efficacy and the precise relevance of the Common Agricultural Policy. The aspirations of member countries where farming is a large-scale operation, such as Britain, are in conflict with those of countries where farming is smaller scale, such as France and the European "south". However, it is acknowledged in Brussels that what they call there the "economic weight" of agriculture is in decline and that, in the light of recognised "inconsistencies", the CAP will have to adjust to new realities and challenges in the years ahead.

In other words, the Eurocrats accept that there are "inconsistencies" in what they are now choosing to call "sustainable rural development". Ironing out these inconsistencies is seen as imperative, as is the need to have sustainable rural development at the top of the EU agenda. Action along these lines, it is said, must underpin all rural policy in the short term, and also after the EU's enlargement.

In this context, it would be nice to think that November 1996 was a pivotal month in the history of European and British ways of dealing with rural deprivation. In that month, all 15 member states, as well as the states waiting in the ante-room of the wider Europe, along with the US, Canada and Japan, sent emissaries to Cork, in Ireland, to discuss future perspectives for rural Europe.

All important developments in Europe, the organisers agreed, were relevant to its rural future: the economy and world trade, the introduction of a single currency and the likely enlargement of the EU itself. Three days of talks led to a suitably ringing declaration under the now familiar title, *A Living Countryside*. "Sustainable rural development," the declaration said, "aims at reversing rural out-migration, combating poverty, stimulating employment and equality of opportunity, and responding to growing requests for more quality, health, safety, personal development and leisure, and improving rural well-being." It went on: "There must be a fairer balance of public spending, infrastructure investments and educational, health and communications services between rural and urban areas. A growing share of available resources should be used for promoting rural development and securing environmental objectives...

"Emphasis must be on participation and a 'bottom up' approach which harnesses the creativity and solidarity of rural communities. Rural development must be local and community driven within a coherent European framework."

In the peroration, it declared that Europe's policy-makers should be urged "to raise public awareness about the importance of making a new start in rural development policy; and to make rural areas more attractive to people to live and work in, and become centres of a more meaningful life for a growing diversity of people of all ages". In such a declaration, inevitably, there was a bit of something for everyone. Doubtless, there are items in it to satisfy one or two unstated hidden agendas from certain participants. Certainly, the British delegation agreed, there was a lot of commonsense in the wording, but also, for some, there were traces of a less acceptable woolly-headed supremacism. It provided yet another opportunity for some British representatives present to give voice to their ambivalence about all things European.

It is this nagging ambivalence, and the political reservations that it has given rise to, that has obscured sight of the EU potential for intervening in, and possibly easing, Britain's particular rural poverty problems. While the existence of that potential is not in doubt, and the financial mechanisms to give aid have occasionally been activated, the fact that poverty and deprivation in England might be eligible for a European "treatment" has had nothing like the airing that many would think appropriate.

In a number of areas, however, the treatment has been taken up, though not without complications on both the British and the EU side. The ability to sustain interest on the part of would-be applicants, and, one suspects, their whole-hearted motivation, seems to be vital in the process of applying to Brussels for funding. Thus, it took "sustained campaigning" on the part of Lincolnshire County Council, for example, when it opted to go for what the Europeans calls Objective 5b status and extra funds for rural development in the county.

It was not an easy option. Before the grant could even be considered, an agreed strategy had to be drawn up, outlining how the money would be spent and what would be achieved. This strategy then needed the endorsement of all interested local authorities in the county, the bigger local employers and at least three government departments. Finally, it had to be approved by both the British Government and the European Commission before the former submitted it to the latter.

Within the framework of its application, Lincolnshire was able to list the following priorities: agricultural diversification and development; tourism; business development; and human resources and communities. Each "priority" had to be accompanied by its own outline of actions to be taken, and the expected outcomes. That part was easy. More difficult, apparently, was the matter of sustaining the willingness of all the parties involved in jumping through the hoops that were erected, as well as the the goodwill in providing matching funding – a crucial EU requirement.

In the end, under Objective 5b (which "facilitates the development and structural adjustment in rural areas"), the county was able to attract nearly £1 million over a three-year period from the European Regional Development Fund (ERDF). The total grant available to the whole of Britain under Objective 5b runs to about £360 million for the five years to the end of 1999.

The ERDF is one of a number of structural funds through which EU financial support is directed for social and economic development in rural areas. In each case, under the principle known as additionality, matching funds have to be found locally. Other possible sources include the European Social Fund (ESC) and the European Agricultural Guidance and Guarantee Fund (EAGGF). Objective 2, which helps to rehabilitate "regions affected by industrial decline", as well as 5b, can be relevant to meeting specific needs in Britain's rural areas.

European funds can be sought for "community initiatives", but these applications too have to be accompanied by "operational programmes" which have to be approved by the British Government of the day and the EU. But the most significant European inititiave for English rural areas is a funding mechanism called LEADER II, which runs for six years until 1999 (succeeding LEADER I, which expired in 1994). Its chief characteristic is that there should be evidence that everyone affected by a project for integrated and sustainable development (in a "living" countryside) will in fact be able to participate.

At the Cork conference, the keynote address came from Franz Fischler, an Austrian agronomist who is EU Commissioner for Agriculture and Rural Development. He spoke with a directness which was refreshing and contrasted sharply with the weary obfuscations coming from British ministers at the time. He also spoke, as a European would, of structural weaknesses in Europe's rural areas – gaps in the infrastructure, lack of jobs, inadequate services and training facilities. "We have no right to sit back and watch this happening," he declared. "We must secure the future of European agriculture ... and all rural development policy must consistently foster the creation of jobs outside agriculture and an improvement in the infrastructure and the range of available services."

He emphasised that the advantages of the bottom-up approach were "self-evident" – something about which few British ministers would then openly enthuse – since they were in line with EU principles of subsidiarity. But these advantages, according to a French participant, were preached more often than they were applied. Jean-François Poncet, a member of the French Senate, urged that there should be what he called a "regional global" programme for all rural areas without exception. With a Gaullist flourish, he announced that there had to be integration, and solidarity as well as diversity.

Away from the podium, there was a familiar ring to pronouncements from the floor. A "well thought out" countryside, said one speaker, could be a place of happiness regained. Ah but, said another, it was essential for human beings to be at the heart of any outside interventions. But, asked a third, what about setting up a European rural fund? (An idea which is intermittently floated whenever rural regeneration comes up for scrutiny.) A fourth warned that the countryside ought not to be "idealised" either by rural or urban people, and that we all had to beware of romantic "neo-ruralism".

Chapter *thirteen*
By Way of Conclusion

*Rural England 1996 sets out a number of quantifiable
targets relevant to rural areas, such as: seeking to double
the levels of cycling by the year 2002, and again by
2112; (and) restoring breeding otters, by 2010, to all
the catchment and coastal areas where they have been
recorded since 1960.*

Rural England 1996
(a Government/Stationery Office publication)

*Concerns have been expressed that cross departmental
targets are merely paper promises.*

Briefing paper for voluntary organisations on
Rural England 1996

for even the most dispassionate of interlocutors, increasing poverty
in the 1980s and 1990s became a political issue. A groundswell of
concern grew, as did poverty itself, during the era of John Major, and
particularly in the run-up to the 1997 general election. As one of
Margaret Thatcher's Cabinet ministers acknowledged – after leaving
her Government – the growth of poverty in her time was "blatant".
The success of New Labour in the 1997 election has nudged the
debate on eradication a little closer to centre stage, though for many

the debate is peppered more with hope than promise.

A lingering equivocation remains in the air. It takes the form of warnings that while the new Government is not without policies to tackle the problem, the constraints on it, and particularly the financial constraints, are such that progress might be slow. More experienced advisers from the political Left remain convinced of the danger of tinkering at the edges when what is required is a full-frontal attack.

But, on the part of the new policy-makers, at least there is evidence of an acute awareness. The mix of Labour and Liberal-Democrat members of Parliament, and especially the new members, has brought a first-hand knowledge of the poverty problem on the ground. There is now a generous sprinkling of ex-local authority members, former schoolteachers, social workers, and – most important, so far as the theme of this book is concerned – of MPs representing rural constituencies. The House of Lords has been similarly re-invigorated, with a Labour infusion of "working peers".

In many of the erstwhile Tory shires, the worm has turned with a vengeance. Suddenly, substantial parts of Sussex, Yorkshire, Lancashire, the Home Counties and Derbyshire – which had been thought Tory fiefdoms – now have Labour or Liberal-Democrat representation. The political landscape of the country, which had been dominated by a Tory inheritance built on old-fashioned class structures, has changed tectonically.

This development means that future debates on poverty, inside the House of Commons as well as outside, will not be so much dominated by the urban or the inner-city experience as they have been in the past. They will also include first-hand evidence of deprivation and disadvantage in the countryside. Given the constraints, it is likely that these debates will have their difficult, even their acrimonious, moments. But no government action can now be taken without some knowledge of what is really happening.

Sociologically, and especially for the countryside, this is a hugely important change. The countryside – like patriotism and, in some accounts, the Church of England – has until now been largely a Conservative domain. The landowners, the squires and, most piquantly, the leading nostalgists have been predominantly of the political Right. What, one wonders, is the political allegiance of those who in recent years have left the towns and cities to settle in the countryside?

The squirearchy has largely disappeared and the land owners, if the upper echelons of the Country Landowners Association are anything to go by, are developing a more articulate social conscience. The class which doffed its cap in deference has almost gone. Even the National Trust is now more concerned than previously with aspects of the social fabric, including the characteristically "ordinary" aspects, as well as big "country houses" and the more predictable areas of outstanding beauty. The Council for the Protection of Rural England deals as much in encroachments of bricks and mortar as it does in preservation *per se*.

There remains, of course, a countryside we all love. Its beauty and its uniqueness are part of all of us. If this book has appeared to look on the gloomy side of life, it is because it is difficult to write about the influences – and the facts – of poverty without being gloomy. But it is not an attempt to deny what is undoubtedly positive and life-enhancing about the rural scene; rather an attempt to put it in perspective. Most people who have spent their lives in the country-side are aware, as some researchers have underlined, of the "spiritual" richness of their surroundings.

But attitudes to the countryside are likely to be even more confused in the next few years. The queues will continue to form outside Dove Cottage in the Lake District, where the Wordsworths lived, while "Hardy country" and the Cotswolds of Laurie Lee are certain to keep their appeal. But will such phenomena keep their place in the political debate any more?

Ironically, it was Stanley Baldwin, the Conservative Prime Minister who crushed the cathartic General Strike of 1926, who was able, in his book *On England*, to express a quintessentially Tory view of the countryside. It is a view which may be dated when it comes to detail, but which coincides with the view of many day trippers, incomers and other escapists as they muse in their armchairs or sit and watch, as millions do, the rurally-based television soaps.

Baldwin, an industrialist's son, described himself as "a son of the soil", and though he spent his public life immersed in politics in the metropolis he remained something of a romantic at heart. England is "the country", he liked to say, and "the country" is England. (Echoes here more recently of another former Prime Minister, John Major, who would probably argue that cricket on the village green and warm beer were England, and even vice versa.)

Asked what most reminded him of England, Baldwin wrote of "the tinkle of the hammer on the anvil in the country smithy, the corncrake on a dewy morning, the sound of the scythe against the whetstone, and the sight of the plough team coming over the brow of a hill, the sight that has been seen in England since England was a land, and may be seen in England long after the Empire has perished and every works in England has ceased to function... These are the things that make England."

Of more recent vintage, but equally lyrical in his turn of phrase, has been Enoch Powell, a controversial intellectual who was also to serve in a Conservative Cabinet. He too could speak with almost poetic eloquence – and he was a some-time poet – of things rural that were precious and important to him and, as he saw it, to the nation. But he was also a politician who was brutally frank, even suicidal from the career point of view, in his views on non-White immigration into the country he loved.

But if the romanticism of the Conservative Party has been eroded by the voters of 1997, the romanticism of the Labour Party is still there to conjure with. It is a reasonable assumption that the early 19th century poet, John Clare, would have voted Labour, or at least New Labour. Certainly, he has been an influence on Left-of-Centre thinking ever since – up to and, presumably, beyond Denis Healey, for instance, who has proclaimed himself a great enthusiast and who now lives in deepest rural Sussex.

Today's Labour and Liberal-Democratic members of Parliament, and their counterparts in local authorities throughout England, carry with them such a legacy. They carry, for example, the thinking of George Lansbury, leader of the Labour Party in the Baldwin era. Though a Londoner through and through, he too could wax lyrical when he wanted to on the state of the English countryside. In 1934, he announced that he longed as much as anything for the reclamation and re-creation of rural England. Was this very longing a presentiment of the demise of something?

Contemporary Labour thinking, not unexpectedly, has been more down to earth. Elliot Morley, a front bench speaker on matters agricultural since 1989 and who was made a junior countryside minister after the 1997 landslide, has spoken of the needs for change in the countryside, especially in the rural economy. In an address to a conference in late 1995 on ways of achieving sustainable community development in the rural areas, he asked for something of everything. A viable economy, adequate services, an integrated approach, including some European input, and much more besides, were included among Labour's political priorities. The proof of the pudding has yet to come, but the romance, for the time being anyway, has been put to one side.

Despite such outwardly promising developments, and despite the facts and the statistics that say everything there is to say about increasing poverty in late 20th century Britain, there is still "an alarming lack of interest" in the subject. The deepening divide between rich and poor, said a Rowntree Foundation paper in May 1997, has been only modestly reduced by public spending on social services, welfare, housing and education.

Even practising social workers have been chastised by one of their most senior representatives. In early 1996, Allan Orrick, chair of the

In Cumbria:
"When it comes to the future, local authorities are very aware, regional government offices not so."

In Buckinghamshire:
"I think policy-makers fight shy of identifying poverty and deprivation. However, there are some exceptions."

In Wiltshire:
"There is no comprehension nationally of the rural perspective. Poverty in an age of affluence is being unable to write and have others write about you."

In Warwickshire:
"From where I stand, the future looks much like the past."

poverty and social justice committee of the British Association of Social Workers, has warned that practitioners were surprisingly uninterested in the subject which is "at the very core" of the problems they deal with. What sort of society, he seemed to be asking, have we become?

The cry from the anti-poverty lobbies remains insistent and familiar to those who know the scene. It is a cry from the heart which is also a reasoned cry from the head. But since, time and again, it has grown used to getting a response from the top which is more rejection than proper response, or at most a quasi-helpless shrug of the shoulders, the cry has to be repeated, time and again. What the lobbies do not articulate, though some of their most ardent supporters feel it strongly, is that something must be done. If nothing is done, they say, then it is not implausible that what passes for the rural idyll could be shattered by manifestations of social unrest not experienced since the last century.

Leading figures in these lobbies still carry with them a formidable but concentrated shopping list. It is a list which is a touch dog-eared because it has been on the table for some time, but it is nevertheless a list of essentials which has to be revisited if tangible progress towards improvement is to be made.

At the top is a call for a nationally-recognised and agreed definition of what constitutes poverty in Britain today. Some definitions do exist, and they have been given in these pages, but "agreement", in the sense of universal endorsement, is missing. To reach agreement entails political as well as semantic compromise, for it is now well known that leading politicians in 1990s Britain have publicly declined to admit that poverty exists.

Once a definition has been achieved, the minimum wage, for a start, has to be legally binding, and there has to be genuine job security. Far too many people in the countryside are forced into doing casual work, in poor conditions and for unacceptably low wages. This means that pay continues to be an area fraught with political complications, but where a new relationship with the European Union (launched with an endorsement of its Social Chapter) should have a decisive influence.

Then, the shopping list goes on, there has to be an end to the gross under-funding for rural areas. A disengaged examination, comparing funds available for regeneration in urban areas with those available, thus far, for the rural areas, would be very instructive.

Also high on the list is a demand for a national strategy which would recognise and would do something to improve the special situation of women among the very poor. Perhaps, it is sometimes argued, this could be accomplished through sensitive community work, but then, the lobbies say, a workable, properly funded community development structure has first to be put in place and established as a permanent fixture.

To secure progress in meeting the list's demands, the challenge has to be met with those – including ministers and some senior civil servants – who insist on seeing poverty as an urban phenomenon which should not be allowed to tarnish perceptions of the rural idyll. Getting the issues of rural poverty accepted, discussed and sensibly addressed, when so many in the population have wanted nothing to do with it, represents a substantial challenge.

The key questions remain: who is to present this challenge, and how? One answer is, of course, the Rural Community Councils. They exist, they have a structure, and they have their own association, in the form of ACRE. But the RCCs are not all the same and they are not all similarly motivated. Some, it is clear, move with more speed and sense of purpose and concern than others. A common cause would clearly galvanise them.

This makes particularly interesting the first tentative steps that were being taken in early 1997 towards the eventual establishment of a national body, which could provisionally be called the rural forum. One suggestion is that such a body would draw in leading figures from the voluntary sector, who would support the case for rural regeneration at local and central government level and, where appropriate, in Europe.

Their proposals for regeneration would focus on real and identified needs for integrated social, economic and environmental improvement and change. Once under way, the processes that it would set in motion would enable rural communities themselves to participate at key stages – in appraisal, where required, and in the forging of inter-sectoral partnerships. Up to a point, rural regeneration programmes can learn from the urban experience.

Supporters of the forum see it as a logical outcome of the work that has been done under the banner of the Rural Poverty Initiative. This was a programme started in early 1995 by ACRE, in conjunction with its partners from among the country's 38 rural community councils who were already pressing for action in this area. They saw it as a problem in their geographical areas and were determined to raise awareness of it. Even in nationally economically straitened circumstances, they said, there had to be more resources for the poor.

ACRE's *raison d'être* and its sense of "mission" – to improve the rural quality of life – have been directly relevant to this exercise. Its efforts to influence government policy, and individual members of Parliament, have been at the heart of the initiative. A number of new research projects have been launched and there has been collaboration with a series of voluntary organisations, such as Age Concern, the Children's Society, the Citizens Advice Bureaux, the Community Development Foundation, Oxfam, and others.

In March 1997, the rationale for the intitiative, and for its continuation, was strengthened by an intervention from a body calling itself the National Local Government Forum Against Poverty. It too demanded unambiguously that there should be nothing less than a "shake-up" in the way funding and "help" were allocated to hard-up rural areas. In yet another study, published at that time, Paul Milbourne and fellow researchers uncovered a picture of continuing frustration being felt by local councils who were doing their limited best to assist and support the deprived.

The frustration arose partly as a result of tight financial restraints imposed, in the forms of "caps" on spending plans, by central government. They had started seriously to impinge on council spending programmes in the early 1990s, leading to acrimonious disputes which, in some instances, reached the High Court. In addition, new curbs were being introduced on local government's statutory powers and, said Milbourne, there was "a failure by central government to recognise the particular nature of rural poverty". Relations between central and local government had reached an all-time low.

The study found that those government-funded regeneration programmes which had been introduced, like the centrally authorised deprivation indicators from which they usually emanated, were too often geared to mainly urban criteria. Inappropriate indicators led, as a consequence, to difficulties in gathering the right data, even where deprivation was clearly present; and, where budgets were tight, there was poor resourcing for essential anti-deprivation programmes. But the team's inescapable conclusion was that while local councils in general wanted to "do something" to tackle poverty, they were hamstrung by central government restrictions.

This team was clearly asking for nothing more nor less than a sea change in official attitudes. Its members were warning, as they had warned before, that the critical moment in the formulation of any programme to tackle rural poverty lies at the very beginning of the operation, when the indicators to be used in measuring and assessing it are being drawn up. It was by now a familiar theme: urban criteria are inappropriate and insensitive in the rural context.

Here, too, as elsewhere, the call is for more exchanges with locally involved people – or, as Milbourne puts it, with carefully chosen local groups. These would have to include individuals who, by their very nature, have rarely felt able to approach local council offices and who have had little to do even with voluntary organisations working on their behalf. The poor and the disadvantaged are often, in their own way, detached – and, for one reason or another, disenfranchised.

Questions of whether and how local councils should pursue their own anti-poverty programmes are frequently contentious and especially difficult in rural areas. Once again, ancillary questions can arise relating to the possibilities of stigma and the wish for confidentiality and anonymity in a small community. The getting and the taking of advice, let alone financial or other material assistance, can be very complex affairs when, by tradition, the reasons why such operations may be necessary have been a closely-guarded secret.

Suffolk County Council, on the other hand, is an authority which in recent years has routinely expressed pride at the way it has accommodated to change in fast-moving times. It is Constable country, squarely on the tourist beat, but it is also a county with higher than average proportions of pensioners below the poverty line, of single parents, and of deprived young couples with children. Even so, it says in its public documents, dealing with poverty must not be an isolated activity. It has to underlie a large part of council services and to be high priority on a consistent and long-term basis.

Caroline Welch, who has researched the circumstances of Suffolk's poor, says she has been driven to conclude that beyond doubt there is a "crisis" in the countryside. But John Gummer, the one-time Environment Minister with a seaside home on the Suffolk coast, made no reference to a "crisis" when launching his supposedly seminal 1995 White Paper on Rural England. Too often the dialogue about poverty in rural England, if and when it has taken place, has been a dialogue of the deaf.

Brian McLaughlin, meanwhile, has urged a complete overhaul rather than just caution in, for instance, the approach to employment problems. One of his concerns has been the growth of the nostalgia industry through the promotion of tourism and heritage. As County Durham turns into Bede County, Exmoor into Lorna Doone Country and Nottingham into Robin Hood County, it becomes increasingly necessary, he says, to look at the quality as well as the quantity of jobs being created. What do we really achieve, he asks, if we continue to create low-paid jobs in a high-cost economy? For McLaughlin, it is a central paradox that "our future in rural areas" is apparently being determined by the most articulate and/or those who can afford the best advocates. One consequence of this will be that "country folk will increasingly be replaced by folk who live in the country". And if that is not a desirable outcome, then policy-makers will need to think quickly about what sort of intervention is required to change it.

Half-a-dozen years on from that McLaughlin prediction, one of the Government's chosen means – presumably – of seeking to change things has been through the controlled munificence of the National Lottery Charities Board. This body was set up in 1995 to distribute funds accruing from Lottery flutters to charitable, benevolent and philanthropic organisations. One of its cardinal aims has been to improve the quality of life for people and communities disadvantaged by poverty. After the first tranche of NLCB funding was distributed, Jonathan Brown, of the National Council for Voluntary Organisations, analysed just how successful rural groups had been in their bids for Lottery support. Between May and July 1995, he found that 30,000 application packs were sent to groups in all parts of the UK and that half of them were duly submitted. A total of 1,824 applicants said their projects were intended to benefit people in rural areas, and 306 of these were successful. Slightly over £12.4 million went to the winning rural applicants. During 1997, the three themes being canvassed by the Lottery organisers for applications were: New Opportunities and Choices; Improving People's Living Environment; and Community Involvement. The NCVO itself, which has a distinctly ambivalent attitude to many of the ramifications and implications of the Lottery, wants refinements under these headings which will, hopefully, encourage more rurally-based applications.

A central purpose of this book has been to question attitudes to rurality, and especially to rural poverty. It may be desirable to preserve what remains of the idyll, because there is so much that is precious about the English countryside. But it must be hugely debatable that the alleviation of poverty – anywhere – should be dependent on the whim of people placing a highly improbable bet.

Chapter *fourteen*
An ABC of Solutions

Such solutions as have been have been sought, attempted and sometimes achieved in rural areas have often been through the rural community councils (RCCs). These bodies – 38 in all, one in each county – have been active in the role of brokers. It is they who have brought together the statutory and the voluntary agencies, as well as, where possible, the private sector, in the name of social and economic regeneration. From all these diverse sources, and from the Rural Development Commission, they get their funding. They are independent charities.

Under the umbrella of ACRE, which is the RCCs' association, the collective stated aim is to keep England's villages alive and thriving. The view is that a village which does not provide any affordable housing for its young people, or which loses its shop, or post office or school, quickly loses its heart and its community life. "All too easily," says ACRE, "it can become a dormitory – attractive, but without a soul." In the following pages, outline details are given of a wide range of projects that have been initiated, with and without the brokerage of the RCCs, to save the souls of some of England's rural communities. It does not include the several county-wide consciousness-raising exercises that have been launched in several parts of the country. This book is in large measure an endorsement of those exercises, even though sometimes they turn out to be a device used by a ruling council to ration out scarce resources even more stringently than before.

Some of these projects have already been referred to in the preceding pages, in which case an extra detail or two has been added. The range does not claim in any way to be exhaustive and it does not claim to have solved every problem that has been touched on. Rather the list should be read perhaps as a compilation of prescriptions and methods drawn from projects which seem to be working for some communities, and which could, with imagination and enthusiasm, provide ideas for others to learn from or copy.

Above all, they are intended to demonstrate that financial input from outside sources, while always welcome and often very useful, is not totally indispensable. What is more important is the knowledge that solutions are possible. In difficult situations, people who may feel marginalised or powerless can achieve more if they have the will, and especially if they find others with the same motivation to try with them.

ADULT EDUCATION Training on Wheels is an outreach adult education project bringing computers, languages and other "new directions" skills to people who are isolated from educational opportunities, but who are living in areas where regeneration is required because traditional industries have declined. Details: Workers' Educational Association in North Yorkshire. Tel: 01757-269157.

BENEFITS, Income support and special allowances are a complicated area, involving much form-filling, and it is rarely simple to work out entitlements. Claims have to be submitted in writing to begin with and then thrashed out at the local Benefits Agency. In remoter areas, this may be a benefits bus (See next item). Income support is a means-tested benefit intended to bring a person's income up to a government-approved minimum. Telephone numbers for the nearest Benefit Inquiry Line, giving general advice and information, can be obtained from most Post Offices, from a Health Visitor, from the Citizens Advice Bureau, or from local Council offices. (See also WELFARE RIGHTS, below).

BENEFITS BUSES are being cut in some areas, but are being developed in others. When they are operating, they carry trained advisers with information on a whole range of Social Security matters. Some have a lift to allow access for people with prams and wheel-chairs. Details: Benefits Agency. Fax: 0532-324135.

CHILDREN The North Cotswold Mobile Project reaches out to parents, carers, childminders, parent-and-toddler groups, etc, in the isolated North Cotswold area. It loans out resources (play and sports equipment), it provides training, parental support, and generally enables increased play opportunities. Working in a large geographical area, it reaches the end of three-year funding (mainly from the non-statutory sector) in March 1998. It remains to be seen whether the statutory authorities will assist in continuing the service. Tel: 01452-528491.

The Oasis Centre – located at Ludgvan County Primary School, Penwith, Cornwall, is a purpose-built community childcare centre, providing affordable, accessible and flexible places for local children aged 2-11 years. It offers playgroup, nursery, before-and-after play school sessions, and holiday schemes. Tel: 01736-740331.

COMMUNITY BUSINESSES These are owned and controlled by members of the community, with the specific aim of benefiting and helping to sustain that community. Suffolk Co-operative and Community Enterprise Support Service (SUCCESS) offers free advice and help. Tel: 0345-660227.

COMMUNITY CARE A county-wide network of village contacts has been started in Nottinghamshire, co-ordinated by a village care officer based at Nottinghamshire Rural Community Council. This officer works with rural communities to ensure that care is accessible to all, and especially the disadvantaged, through the provision of information, advice, support and training for volunteers. Care groups offer varied services – from collecting prescriptions and other shopping to transport to surgery, hospital, or drop-in centre. Outings and respite care can be arranged. Tel: 01636-815267.

COMPUTER ADVICE LINK LINE (CALL) Based in libraries, but also available in post offices, health centres and village halls throughout rural Cornwall, it gives access to several thousand records, with information on local councils, leisure activities, training courses and care in the community resources. Tel: 01872-272702.

COMPUTER LIBRARY LINK Norfolk Library and Information Service provides libraries in three village shops in the west of the county. Each shop carries its own stock of books and a terminal with dial-up access to the library service computer system through which book reservations can be made. In some areas, shop libraries are seen as more cost effective than mobile library services. Tel: 01603-223900.

CORT (Consortium of Rural TECs) is an independent body set up in 1991 to assist in the development and regeneration of rural economies and communities. Working with partners from the statutory, voluntary and private sector (eg, Chambers of Commerce) it seeks to influence regional, national and EU policies. In May 1997, it had 25 member TECs and eight associate members. Tel: 0116-254 4166.

CREDIT UNIONS These started in Germany in the 19th century, and in Britain are regulated by a 1979 Act of Parliament. They are financial co-operatives, owned and controlled by their members, mostly volunteers, and are described by them as ethical and accountable alternative ways of saving and borrowing. Estimates are that nearly £2 billion are lost every year in interest charges in rural England – levied by loan sharks and the big banks. But with credit unions, generated profits are distributed among members, while the interest charged on loans is fixed, by law, at a maximum of one per cent a month. Money is retained in the community, where it is most needed. Repayments are usually tailored to suit the borrower's needs. Details: Association of British Credit Unions. Tel: 0161-832 3694.

ELECTRONIC VILLAGE HALL At Newcastle-on-Clun, South Shropshire, a newly-equipped community centre includes its own "electronic village hall". This houses computers for word processing, account-keeping, and access to local education and job opportunities. Launched in August 1996, a network of similar centres is expected to follow. Tel: 01588-640168.

FOYERS were introduced into France in the 1950s and into Britain in 1992. The aim is to provide homeless young people with accommodation, training and employment opportunities – under one roof. The Foyer Federation works specifically in areas where affordable homes are most hard to find, and some offer help for drugs and alcohol abusers. An objective is to have 400 foyers nation-wide by the year 2002. Details: 0171-377 5847.

Mobile foyers, financed in part by the Rural Development Commission, are active in some rural areas. Computers are available and help is given with form filling and job applications. Job cards from local JobCentres are carried. A successful scheme is currently operating in remoter villages in North Yorkshire. Details: 01748-825752.

HOUSEBOUND SHOPPERS' SERVICE Launched in Cambridge for pensioners and disabled people, who telephone their orders to the local Co-op, which works with St John's Ambulance Volunteers – as shoppers – to ensure same-day delivery. Details: 01284-701743.

HOUSING A range of organisations and groups seek to promote social housing and related schemes in rural communities. Some examples follow:-

ACRE (Action with Communities in Rural England) It has a network of Rural Community Councils (RCCs) and, with them, it supports village initiatives including housing aid services (for example, in Derbyshire, Gloucestershire and Hertfordshire); new housing schemes (for example, in Warwickshire and Wiltshire); and, on a pilot basis, housing "enabler" projects in Devon, Lincolnshire, Northumberland, Sussex and Yorkshire – leading to the Rural Development Commission's Enabler Initiative (See below). Details: 01285-653477.

HEART (Housing, Employment and Rural Training) operates in Suffolk to encourage self-help among young people and to reverse the spiral of no work, no home, no prospects. It is seeking to acquire redundant buildings in selected market towns to serve as bases for providing local young people with life skills and social skills centres. Details: 01728-724711.

Housing Enablers' Initiative was established by the RDC, following ACRE's pilot scheme, in 1996. Its purpose is to "facilitate the increased supply of affordable rural housing by helping to speed up the planning and pre-development stages of rural housing schemes, and by assisting, where appropriate, with the development of schemes, and by encouraging and facilitating the return of empty properties into use". In addition, the RDC part-funds a whole range local projects. Details: 0171-340 2900.

Options is another RDC initiative. Through the formation of "land banks", it seeks to bring forward and secure sites for rural social housing schemes. In April 1997, for example, the Sussex Options land bank was able to announce a scheme for just two houses in the village of Twineham, developed by Hyde Housing Association. Details: 0171-340 2900.

The Rural Housing Trust is a charity founded in 1976 to help and advise parish and district councils on how to measure housing need and find suitable sites, and to advise landowners wishing to make land available for housing. The trust's motivation, in its own words, is that the English village way of life is under threat, and that the lifeblood of many villages is being forced out as local house prices climb. Details: 0171-0793 8114.

ICOM (Industrial Common Ownership Movement) is a national organisation whose members are co-operatives or other employee-controlled organisations. It provides training programmes, publications, and gives advice on legal and EU matters. Details: 0113-246 1738.

LETS is the Local Exchange Trading System, a scheme which was was introduced to Britain (from Canada) in 1985. They give everyone a chance to do something practical for themselves and their communities by exchanging goods and skills, listed in a local directory. No money, tokens or certificates are involved, only recorded debits and credits of individuals' available skills, goods and services. These may be "bought" and "sold" and "cheque books" may be used, but the LETS currency stays in the community. Anyone can join or start a LETS system; practitioners claim it is more flexible than barter, and does not affect benefits or tax. It can widen social networks and can give new strength to the local community while also enhancing individual self-esteem. They can be used to support the learning of new skills, stemming unemployment and poverty. Details: (North of England) 0161-434 8712; (South of England) 01909-352848. LETSlink: 01985-217871.

"MOBILES" In the rural context, these may be converted buses, library vans or ambulances, which have been converted after consultation with interested young people on what would be appropriate to meet their needs. They can be used to take them on outings, or for educational or other (lighter) projects of their choice. Some, on longer trips, have been used as living quarters. More than a hundred now exist, run with backing from local youth groups and support from the National Youth Agency. Details: 0116-285 6789.

MULTI-FUNCTIONAL CENTRES These may be housed in redundant community buildings (such as schools or hospitals) which have been converted to house a range of activities and services. In Chipping Norton, Oxfordshire, an old school building now has creche facilities, after-school and holiday play schemes, a family centre, adult education classes, and a computer training centre. It also provides a meeting place for all sorts of voluntary groups, a toy library, a disability support group, and credit union development group. Grants were obtained from the RDC and the County Council. Up to 10 new jobs were created to staff the centre. Details: 01608-644440.

POST A 7.3 tonne lorry, converted into a mobile post office, has been on trial, serving 10 villages in remoter parts of North and East Cumbria. Details: Post Office Counters Ltd. Tel: 0850-913810.

PRA (Participatory Rural Appraisal) networking has been developed in the rural areas of East Yorkshire. Training courses, emphasising the importance of bottom-up developments and strictly voluntary participation, have been so successful that more are having to be organised. Details: 01482-883783.

RACISM Rural England has been multi-racial at least since the 16th century, but a report from the Commission for Racial Equality, *Keep Them in Birmingham* (1995), found that racial discrimination and prejudice were rife in a number of areas. Researchers have also found that explicitly racist political parties have been active, as agitators and as recruiters, in some rural areas. One consequence has been the setting-up of the Rural Anti-Racism Project (RARP) by the National Council for Voluntary Organisations. RARP's aim is to establish race equality policies and practices with organisations and decision-making individuals in rural areas. Staff at RARP's race equality office are happy to exchange thoughts and ideas with interested parties. Details: 0171-713 6161.

RURAL ACTION for the Environment supports community-led action, preferably with an environmental element. Community groups can apply for project grants of up to £2,000 to pay for specialist advice, skills training, etc. The grants are RCC-administered in each county, with sponsorship from the RDC, the Countryside Commission and English Nature. In Crediton, mid-Devon, a group based at the local volunteer centre obtained Rural Action funding for a feasability study into refurbishing donated household furniture for use by hard-up local families. This study led to secure initial funding from the district council and from Agenda 21, and became operational in October 1996. It is run by unemployed volunteers and achieved its short-term aims, outgrowing its first premises, within six months. Expansion is now planned to cover a much wider area. It is one of more than 3,000 Rural Action-supported projects to have taken off since October 1992. Details: 01285-659599.

SHOPS, ETC The Horseshoes Inn, Silk Willoughby, near Sleaford, Lincolnshire, secured a redundant building grant from the RDC and converted a former stable into a village shop/post office.

The village shop at Itteringham, Norfolk, was threatened with closure when its keeper died. A Community Shop Association was formed, secured a £4,000 grant, and now runs the shop. Details: 0171-340 2900.

SOCIAL SERVICES and **VOLUNTEERS** Somerset social services department has pioneered a close working partnership with locally-recruited volunteers. In March 1997, its service users were in touch with more than 1,800 of them, with recruitment, training and support co-ordinated by local Voluntary Service Organisations (VSOs). Community Service Volunteers (CSV) groups are used by the county in residential child care units. Details: 0800-317220.

STRESS The Rural Stress Information Network is a relatively new partnership between rural industries, the voluntary sector and government. It was set up in response to high stress, and sometimes suicide, among the farming community, but now covers all people in rural areas. It will provide information and advice on the sources of stress and on initiatives to help in its alleviation. Details: 01203-412916.

TELECOTTAGES These are also known as telecentres or resource centres, and provide local access to computers and telecommunications, training and help in the running of small businesses, including one-person businesses. There are more than 140 in Britain – run by a variety of organisations, from schools to private businesses. Details on their location are obtainable from the Telework, Telecottage and Telecentre Association (TTCA), which was set up in 1993 to encourage teleworking – the practice of working remotely from an employer, and usually handling and transmitting the work electronically. In addition to cottages, the TTCA has more than 2,000 individual members, publishes its own materials, operates a helpline, assists in vocational training, and produces an electronic newsletter. Details: Freephone 0800-616 008.

TRAVELLERS The Friends, Families and Travellers Support Group (FFT) was set up in 1995 to give advice on sites, planning and housing, legal problems, benefit matters, education and health. Details: 01458-832371. Another group, providing similar services, is the Gypsy Council for Education, Culture, Welfare and Civil Rights. Details: 01708-868986.

WELFARE RIGHTS A project targeting rural poverty in North Nottinghamshire raised almost £500,000 in the year to April 1996 for claimants in isolated and deprived fomer coalfield areas. It involved sending a leaflet offering independent benefit advice to every household in the area. Results of the take-up campaign showed there was much under-claiming, leaving people struggling to pay rents or mortgages, heating and fuel bills. Bassetlaw Rural Coalfield Welfare Rights Project is a joint venture of Nottinghamshire Rural Community Council and the county's Welfare Rights Service, with funding from the County Council and the RDC. Details: 01636-815267, or 01623-845016.

YOUTH Somerset Rural Youth Project sets out, with the backing of several local district councils and other interested bodies, to develop initiatives and services which will get young people involved in all aspects of parish and village life. Details: 01823-255727.

References

Chapter *One*

The description of the English landscape as "mankind's supreme contribution to the beauty of this planet" is from Marcus Binney's book, *Legacy, The Changing Face of Landscape*, published by Cape, London, in 1990.

May Molteno's interviews in a small village were brought together and published by Wiltshire Community Council in 1993. They constitute a fascinating portrait of a small community at that time.

The Countryside Commission generally maintains a no-nonsense but wholesome view of "the countryside" as we would all like it to be. This extract is from a 1996 issue of their newspaper, *Countryside*.

Lifestyles in Rural England, published by the Rural Development Commission (RDC) in 1994, has the stamp of authority and was compiled by Paul Cloke, Paul Milbourne and Chris Thomas. I have drawn on its findings many times in this book, and I am very grateful.

Marion Shoard is something of an *enfant terrible* in her attitudes to the countryside, environment, and so on. Like her or not, she is invariably a good read, and *The Theft of the Countryside*, published by Temple Smith, London, in 1980, quoted here, is no exception.

The Conservative Government's White Paper of 1995, called *Rural England: A Nation Committed to a Living Countryside*, was billed as seminal. In a way, it was; but it was also heavily charged with political wishful thinking and provoked much criticism from the grassroots.

Chapter *Two*

L.A. Clarkson's book, *The Pre-Industrial Economy in England*, published by Batsford in London in 1971, has some highly-readable pages. I am grateful for permission to use his material in this chapter.

To define inequality as "a stimulant to competition" may seem distasteful to some. But it was widely-held view on the political Right in the early 1990s. This line is drawn from *The Price of Social Exclusion*, a discussion paper published in 1995 by the then National Federation of Housing Associations (now The National Housing Federation), but by no means endorsed by them.

The second point, about the "dogma" relating to the unemployed, is taken from *Dancing With Dogma*, a seminal account of the Thatcher years, by Ian Gilmour, published by Simon and Schuster in 1992. The author was a Tory MP for 30 years and for some of them a Thatcher minister.

The Child Poverty Action Group does excellent lobbying work behalf of the poor. *Poverty: The Facts*, by Carey Oppenheim and Lisa Harker, was published by the CPAG in 1993 and is exactly what it says it is – the facts. An updated version appeared in 1996.

Social Work, Poverty and Debt, published by the British Association of Social Workers in 1997, is a short but thorough attempt to define social work attitudes. As the editors note, not much work has been done in this area, so it is a welcome contribution.

The decade after the Second World War brought many books on the countryside. Many were nostalgist; some were not. Victor Bonham-Carter's *The English Village* (Penguin Books, London, 1952) was a sensitive and sensible contribution.

Peter Townsend remains one of Britain's most highly-regarded and more radical social scientists. *Poverty in the UK*, one of a number of books he has written on the subject, was published by Penguin in London in 1979. He returned to the subject, very succinctly, in *A Poor Future*, published by Lemos & Crane, London, in 1997.

Francis of Assissi was invoked by Margaret Thatcher on the steps of 10 Downing Street after her general election victory in 1983. It heralded a new era of change and, for many, an era of no hope.

Paul Milbourne and the Countryside Research Unit, part of the Cheltenham College of Further Education, have done much investigative work in the West Country. *Beyond the Village Green*, by Milbourne and Jenny Carson, was published by the college in March 1997 in conjunction with a number of local authorities, ACRE and Oxfam.

Elaine Kempson has managed, very skilfully, to get inside the skin of the poor. She talks and writes with real compassion. Her book, *Hard Times*, was published by the Policy Studies Institute, London, in 1994.

Brian McLaughlin has done for the rural poor what Elaine Kempson has done for the poor of the inner city – researched deeply and sensitively and reached sensible, if controversial, conclusions. Some of his work has been published, most notably *Popular Images and the Reality of Deprivation in Rural Areas*, published by the Arkleton Trust, now part of Aberdeen University, in 1990 (see also under Chapter Eight below).

Chapter *Three*

Graham Harvey's book, *The Killing of the Countryside*, was published by Jonathan Cape, London, in early 1997. Almost every page is as angry as its title.

The validity of the criteria used by Whitehall for measuring rural poverty are increasingly being questioned. The questions here were asked by Rita Hale and Associates, and published by the RDC in 1996.

The Standard Spending Assessment figures are the Government's own.

The National Council for Voluntary Organisations has some very astute poverty watchers. *The Case for a Rural Premium?*, by Jenny Gould, was published by the NCVO in 1995.

Chapter *Four*

Paul Milbourne, see Chapter Two above.

Discussion of employment patterns based on *Unemployment and the Labour Market in the RDAs*, by Christina Beatty and Stephen Fothergill, published by the RDC in February 1997.

Unemployment and the Future of Work was published in London by the Council of Churches for Britain and Ireland, in April 1997. *Faith in the Countryside* was published in 1990.

May Molteno, see Chapter One above.

CPAG, see Chapter Two above.

The London School of Economics' independent research group is the Centre for Economic Performance, and the group's paper, *Jobs, Wages and Poverty*, was published in January 1997.

Tourism jobs figures from the Countryside Commission's journal, *Countryside*, 1996.

Chapter *Five*

Help the Aged has done much valuable research. It is based in London.

Real incomes figures from Department of Social Security publications, available from the Stationery Office.

CPAG, see Chapter Two above.

Brian McLaughlin, see Chapter Two above.

Lifestyles, see Chapter One above.

Statistics on numbers of farm workers from the Rural Agricultural and Allied Workers Group, at the Transport and General Workers Union, London.

Faith in the Countryside, see Chapter Four above.

Discussion of discrimination against rural mothers is prompted by a Rowntree Foundation Social Research Paper, No 108, published December 1996.

Elaine Kempson, writing in *Community Care* magazine, August 29, 1996.

Facts on nutrition from NCH Action for Children, London.

Janet Hemsley reported her findings in the RDC journal, *Rural Focus*, in February 1996.

The RDC guide to childcare practice was written by Jean Scott, of the Kids Club Network.

Childcare places information from a Daycare Trust Briefing Paper, No 1, published in London in 1997.

Poverty in West Cornwall, briefing paper from the School for Policy Studies, Bristol University.

Lifestyles, see Chapter One above.

Fiona, Jenny and Cathy are quoted in *Same Scenery – Different Lifestyle*, a very revealing publication (early 1997) from the Church of England Children's Society, London.

Young people's problems are efficiently discussed in *Nothing Ever Happens Around Here*, published (1994) by the National Youth Agency, Leicester.

Age Concern, the Anchor Trust, and Help the Aged have all published informative documents on care for older people.

Criticisms of the Community Care Act were examined by Ann Davis and Becky Clark, in their report, *Social Work, Poverty and Debt*, published in early 1997 by the British Association of Social Workers, Birmingham.

The English House Condition Survey is published periodically by the Department of the Environment. It is invariably interesting, but invariably out of date.

Chapter *Six*

The Occasional Paper No. 7 was published in 1995 by the Royal College of General Practitioners, London

The allocation of care resources in rural areas has been discussed, in specialist journals and elsewhere, by Ian Watt and others. His and their thoughts here are from *Rural Deprivation, Rural Health and Social Needs in Herefordshire*, published in February 1996.

Dr Watt again – this time in an article for the *Journal of Epidemiology and Community Health*, in 1994.

The reference to the draining of parental energy comes from a report jointly produced by Scope and the North Warwickshire Council for Voluntary Services, at the end of 1995.

The Department of Health paper was called *Developing Health and Social Care in Rural England*, published by the Stationery Office, 1996.

Costs of providing rural health care have been discused in a 1990 NCVO paper, *Counting the Rural Cost*, by S. Wollett.

The survey of the work of professionals with community mental health teams is taken from *A Burden Too Heavy*, published by the Matthew Trust, London SW6, in early 1997.

Chapter *Seven*

The Citizens Advice Bureaux and Norfolk Money Advice have both published valuable documents on rural problem-solving in the last few years.

A detailed and readable account by June Statham and Claire Cameron of the workings of the 1989 Children Act, especially in respect of children under eight in rural areas, was published in the journal, *Children and Society*, in 1994.

The Housing Corporation's Annual Review (1996-97) sets out its targets for rural housing associations.

Chapter *Eight*

Thomas Hardy was a penetrating observer of rural life, but The *Woodlanders* is one of his more complex novels.

Statistics for population movements are drawn from studies published by the Economic and Social Research Council, London, December 1996.

The Countryside in Question, by Howard Newby, was published by Hutchinson, London, in 1988.

The blast from the ever-industrious CPRE was entitled *Rural Roulette*, published by head office in London in late 1996.

The Rural Development Commission publications list is obtainable from 141 Castle Street, Salisbury, Wiltshire (tel: 01722-336255).

The New Economics Foundation, determinedly innovative in its thinking on British institutions, is based in London's East End.

Service availability figures (transport, schools, etc) are from the RDC.

Brian McLaughlin's *Popular Images and the Reality of Deprivation in Rural Areas* was published by the Arkleton Trust, now part of Aberdeen University, in 1990.

Chapter *Nine*

Reconstituting Rurality, by Jonathan Murdoch and Terry Marsden (UCL Press, London, 1996) is cerebral and radical, but very informative.

Howard Newby is one of the most informed, stimulating and gently humorous, writers on the British countryside. These thoughts are borrowed, with gratitude, from his early book, *Green and Pleasant Land?*, published by Hutchinson, London, in 1979.

The treatise, *Conflict and Change in the English Countryside*, by G.M. Robinson, from which I have drawn this definition of *Gemeinschaft*, was published in London by Belhaven in 1990.

The Nicholson quotes are from *Hansard*.

Chapter *Ten*

Images magazine is published by the Foyer Federation, London.

Once again, the CPRE (see above) hits a bull's eye. These projections are from its publication, *Household Growth, Where Shall We Live?*, which appeared in December 1996, in the wake of the Government's own White Paper, *Our Future Homes*.

Newby, see Chapter Seven above.

Murdoch and Marsden, see Chapter Nine above.

The Gypsy and the State, by Derek Scott and Barbara Perez, published by Bristol University in 1995, is an excellent account of what it means to belong to a vulnerable minority in present-day England. The Derbyshire report appeared in the *Derbyshire Times*, 31 October 1996.

The Scottish experience was described in a Rowntree Foundation Housing Research Paper, No 201, published in December 1996.

May Molteno, op.cit.

Helen Sudlow was extremely helpful to me in this section, allowing me to dip freely into an MSc thesis she submitted to the University of Wales College of

Medicine and the Institute of Health Promotion, Cardiff, in 1993.
Shelter's account of a debate it had organised on housing needs and
housing provision was published by its Bristol office in 1996.

Chapter *Eleven*

Country Life magazine must be well known to any reader who has been more
than five minutes in a doctor's or dentist's waiting room. This quotation
appears because it was rather unexpected.
Self-Help in Rural Areas – Is It Different? was an Occasional Paper (No 2)
published in 1988 by the Tavistock Institute for Human Relations,
London. The lengthy but interesting answer to its own question is Yes.
Teresa Cresswell, like Helen Sudlow (see Chapter Ten above), was very helpful. She published her views and experiences in the journal *Development and
Practice*, Vol. 6, No 1, in 1996. So too was Tilly Sellers, of Hull University,
who, writing on behalf of the East Yorkshire PRA Network, provided me
with a full personal memorandum on the subject.

Chapter *Twelve*

The EU view of regional poverty in Britain came from its statistical office,
Eurostat. Some details appeared in the *Local Government Chronicle*, London,
on May 8, 1997.
Details of the EU conference in Cork on rural questions was published by
the Rural Development Commission, London, in late 1996.

Chapter *Thirteen*

Rural England 1996 was a government discussion paper, and an attempt to
keep faith with its predecessor, *Rural England*, which it published in 1995.
It was similarly glossy and similarly sparse when it came to actions (as
opposed to words).
Ian Gilmour again; see note on his book under Chapter Two above. His
chapter on poverty – surprisingly, for a Conservative account – is one of
the longest in the book.
Both Baldwin and Powell, and George Lansbury, are quoted in Martin
Wiener's *English Culture and the Decline of the Industrial Spirit*, first pub-
lished by Cambridge University Press in the US in 1981. The book's title
may be ponderous, but the content is fascinating and insightful from start
to finish.
Alan Orrick was quoted in the February 1996 issue of *Professional Social
Work*, the very sound journal of the British Association of Social Workers.
This frustration of local government was treated in some depth by Paul
Milbourne and others in *Beyond the Village Green* (see Chapter Two above).
Brian McLaughlin's *Popular Images* (see note under Chapter Two above).

Useful Names and Addresses

(Some national organisations have local branches; check with the nearest library, or telephone directory inquiries.)

ACRE (Action with Communities in Rural England), Somerford Court, Somerford Road, Cirencester, Glos GL7 1TW. Tel: 01285-653477.

Age Concern England, 1268 London Road, London SW16 4ER. Tel: 0181-679 8000.

Agricultural and Allied Workers Group, at Transport and General Workers' Union, 16 Palace Street, London SW1E 5JD. Tel: 0171-828 7788.

Alcoholics Anonymous, PO Box 1, Stonebow House, York. Tel: 01904-644026.

ATD Fourth World, 48 Addington Square, London SE5 7LB. Tel: 0171-703 3231.

Carers' National Association, 20-25 Glasshouse Yard, London EC1A 4JS. Tel: 0171-490-8818.

Child Poverty Action Group, 1-5 Bath Street, London EC1V 9PY. Tel: 0171-253 3406.

Church Action on Poverty, Central Buildings, Oldham Street, Manchester M1 1JT. Tel: 0161-236 9321.

Commission for Racial Equality, Elliott House, London SW1E 5EH. Tel: 0171-828 7022.

Community Development Foundation, 60 Highbury Grove, London N5 2AG. Tel: 0171-226 5375.

Consortium of Rural TECs (CORT), 12 York Road, Leicester LE1 5TS. Tel: 0116-254 4166.

Contact-a-Family, 170 Tottenham Court Road, London W1P 0HA. Write, with stamped, addressed envelope.

Equal Opportunities Commission, Overseas House, Quay Street, Manchester M3 3HN. Tel: 0161-833 9244.

Family Fund, PO Box 50, York YO1 2ZX. Tel: 01904-621115.

Family Service Units, 207 Old Marylebone Road, London NW1 5QP. Tel: 0171-402 5175.

Family Welfare Association, 501-505 Kingsland Road, London E8 4AU. Tel: 0171-254 6251.

Foyer Federation for Youth, 91 Brick Lane, London E1 6QL. Tel: 0171-377 9789.

Gingerbread, 35 Wellington Street, London WC2E 7BN. Tel: 0171-240 0953.

Help the Aged, St James's Walk, Clerkenwell Green, London EC1R 0BE. Tel: 0171-253 0253.

Housing Associations Charitable Trust, Yeoman House, 168-172 Old Street, London EC1V 9BP. Tel: 0171-336 7969.

ICOM (Industrial Common Ownership Movement), 20 Central Road, Leeds LS1 6DE. Tel: 0113-246 1738.

Local Government Anti-Poverty Unit, 76-86 Turnmill Street, London EC1M 5QU. Tel: 0171-296 6620.

Low Pay Unit, 27 Amwell Street, London EC1R 1UN. Tel: 0171-713 7616.

MENCAP (Royal Society for Mentally Handicapped Children and Adults), 123 Golden Lane, London EC1Y 0RT. Tel: 0171-454 0454.

MIND (National Association for Mental Health), Granta House, 15-19 Broadway, London E15 4BQ. Tel: 0181-519 2122.

NCH Action for Children, 85 Highbury Park, London N5 1UD. Tel: 0171-226 2033.

National Association of Citizens Advice Bureaux, Myddleton House, 115-123 Pentonville Road, London N1 9LZ. Tel: 0171-833 2181.

National Association of Toy Libraries, 68 Churchway, London NW1 1LT. Tel: 0171-387 9592.

National Childminding Association, 8 Masons Hill, Bromley, Kent BR2 9EY. Tel: 0181-464 6164.

National Council for One-Parent Families, 255 Kentish Town Road, London NW5 2LX. Tel: 0171-267 1361.

National Council for Hospice and Palliative Care Services, Heron House, 322 High Holborn, London WC1V 7PW. Tel: 0171-269 4550.

National Council for Voluntary Organisations, 8 All Saints Street, London N1 9RL. Tel: 0171-713 6161.

National Farmers' Union, 164 Shaftesbury Avenue, London WC2H 8HL. Tel: 0171-331 7200.

National Homeless Alliance, 5-15 Cromer Street, London WC1H 8LS. Tel: 0171-833 2071.

National Lottery Charities Board, 30 Orange Street, London WC2H 7HH. Tel: 0171-747 5299.

National Playbus Association, 93 Whitby Road, Bristol BS4 3QF. Tel: 0117-977 5375.

National Youth Agency, 17-23 Albion Street, Leicester LE1 6GD. Tel: 0116-285 6789.

Oxfam, 274 Banbury Road, Oxford OX2 7DZ. Tel: 01865-311311.

Peak District Rural Deprivation Forum, Hope Clinic, Eccles Close, Hope, Derbys S33 6RG. Tel: 01433-621822.

Pre-School Learning Alliance, 69 King's Cross Road, London WC1X 9LL. Tel: 0171-833 0991.

Royal Association for Disability and Rehabilitation (RADAR), Unit 12, 250 City Road, London EC1V 8AF. Tel: 0171-250 3222.

Relate, National Marriage Guidance, Little Church Street, Rugby, Warwicks CV21 3AP. Tel: 01788-573241.

Rowntree Foundation, 40 Water End, York YO3 6LP. Tel: 01904-629241.

Rural Development Commission, 19 Dacre Street, London SW1H 0DH. Tel: 0171-340 2900.

Rural Stress Information Network, Arthur Rank Centre, Stoneleigh Park, Warwicks CV8 2LZ. Tel: 01203-412916.

Samaritans, 10 The Grove, Slough, Berks SL1 1QP. Tel: 01753-532713.

Save the Children, 17 Grove Lane, London SE5 8RD. Tel: 0171-703 5400.

Shared Care UK, 3 Priory Road, Bristol BS8 1TX. Tel: 01179-467230.

Shelter, 88 Old Street, London EC1V 9HU. Tel: 0171-253 0202.

Unemployment Unit, contactable at address/telephone number of Low Pay Unit (see above).

Women Returners' Network, 8 John Adam Street, London WC2N 6EZ. Tel: 0171-839 8188.

RURAL COMMUNITY COUNCILS:
Members of ACRE marked (A)

(A) **Community Action**, Church House, 74 Long Ashton Road, Long Ashton, Bristol BS18 9LE. Tel: 01275-393837.

(A) **Bedfordshire Rural Communities Charity**, The Old School, Southill Road, Cardington, Bedford MK44 3SX. Tel: 01234-838771.

(A) **Community Council for Berkshire**, Epping House, 55 Russell Street, RG1 7XG. Tel: 0118-961 2000.

(A) **Buckinghamshire Council for Voluntary Service**, Chiltern House, Oxford Road, Aylesbury, Bucks HP19 3EQ. Tel: 01296-21036.

(A) **Cambridgeshire ACRE**, 218 High Street, Cottenham, Cambridge CB4 4RZ. 01954-250144.

Cheshire Community Council, 96 Lower Bridge Street, Chester CH1 1RU. Tel: 01244-322188.

(A) **Cornwall Rural Community Council**, 9a River Street, Truro, Cornwall TR1 2SQ. Tel: 01872-273952.

Voluntary Action Cumbria, The Old Stables, Redhills, Penrith, Cumbria CA11 0DT. Tel: 01768-868086.

(A) **Derbyshire Rural Community Council**, Church Street, Wirksworth, Derbys DE4 4EY. Tel: 01629-824797.

(A) **Community Council of Devon**, County Hall, Topsham Road, Exeter EX2 4QD. Tel: 01392-382533.

(A) **Dorset Community Action**, 57 High Street West, Dorchester DT1 1UT. Tel: 01305-262270.

Durham Rural Community Council, Park House, Station Road, Lanchester, Durham DH7 0EX. Tel: 01207-529621.

(A) **Rural Community Council of Essex**, Mackmurdo House, 79 Springfield Road, Chelmsford CM2 6JG. Tel: 01245-352046.

(A) **Gloucestershire Rural Community Council**, Community House, 15 College Green, Gloucester GL1 2LZ. Tel: 01452-528491.

(A) **Hampshire Council of Community Service**, Beaconsfield House, Andover Road, Winchester SO22 6AT. Tel: 01962-854971.

(A) **Community Council of Hereford and Worcester**, Great Malvern Station, Station Approach, Malvern, Worcs WR14 3AU. Tel: 01684-573334.

(A) **Community Development Agency for Hertfordshire**, 2 Townsend Avenue, St Albans AL1 3SG. Tel: 01727-852298.

(A) **Humber and Wolds Rural Community Council**, 14 Market Place, Howden, Goole, North Humberside DN14 7BJ. Tel: 01430-430904.

(A) **Isle of Wight Rural Community Council**, Read's Posting House, 24 Holyrood Street, Newport, Isle of Wight PO30 5AZ. Tel: 01983-524058.

(A) **Kent Rural Community Council**, 15 Manor Road, Folkestone CT20 2AH. Tel: 01303-850816.

(A) **Community Council of Lancashire**, 15 Victoria Road, Fulwood, Preston PR2 4PS. Tel: 01772-717461.

(A) **Leicestershire Rural Community Council**, Community House, 133 Loughborough Road, Leicester LE4 5LQ. Tel: 0116-266 2905.

Community Council of Lincolnshire, Church Lane, Sleaford, Lincs NG34 7DF. Tel: 01529-302466.

(A) **Norfolk Rural Community Council**, 20 Market Place, Hingham, Norfolk NR9 4AF. Tel: 01953-851418.

(A) **Northamptonshire ACRE, Hunsbury Hill Centre**, Harksome Hill, Northants NN4 9QX. Tel: 01604-765888.

(A) **Nottinghamshire Rural Community Council**, Minster Chambers, Church Street, Southwell NG25 0HD. Tel: 01636-815267.

Community Council of Northumberland, Tower Buildings, 9 Oldgate, Morpeth NE61 1PY. Tel: 01670-517718.

(A) **Oxfordshire Rural Community Council**, Jericho Farm, Worton, Witney, Oxon OX8 1EB. Tel: 01865-883488.

Community Council of Shropshire, 1 College Hill, Shrewsbury SY1 1LT. Tel: 01743-360641.

(A) **Community Council for Somerset**, Victoria House, Victoria Street, Taunton, Somerset TA1 3JZ. Tel: 01823-331222.

Community Council of Staffordshire, Friars Mill, Friars Terrace, Stafford ST17 4DX. Tel: 01785-242525.

(A) **Suffolk ACRE**, Alexandra House, Rope Walk, Ipswich IP4 1LZ. Tel: 01473-584595.

(A) **Surrey Voluntary Service Council**, Astolat, Coniers Way, New Inn Lane, Burpham, Guildford, Surrey GU4 7HL. Tel: 01483-566072.

(A) **Sussex Rural Community Council**, Sussex House, 212 High Street, Lewes BN7 2NH. Tel: 01273-473422.

(A) **Teesside Council for Voluntary Service**, New Exchange Buildings, Queens Square, Middlesbrough TS2 1AA. Tel: 01642-240651.

(A) **Warwickshire Rural Community Council**, The Abbotsford, 10 Market Place, Warwick CV34 4SL. Tel: 01926-499596.

(A) **Community Council for Wiltshire**, Wyndhams, St Joseph's Place, Bath Road, Devizes SN10 1DD. Tel: 01380-722475.

Yorkshire Rural Community Council, William House, Shipton Road, Skelton, York YO3 6XW. Tel: 01904-645271.

Index